Awaken Your Magic

Real Life Manifestation Journeys

Compiled By Kyra Schaefer

Contents

Chapter 1

Fulfilling the Thirteen-Year Soulmate Prophecy

By Christina Bellevue

Amid the vibrant energy of downtown Toronto, there I was, a young woman in the bloom of her late twenties, standing at a turning point in my life and hungry for transformation. This narrative is like a rich tapestry, intricately woven with strands of desire, destined paths, faith, and the enchanting magic of manifestation. This is a true story born from a courageous choice to reshape my life's story, and my desire to attract a legendary love and live an extraordinary life.

I remember the day vividly. It was a moment filled with desperation and trepidation. I was on my way to meet an astrologer, a man named Allen, who seemed to hold the keys to understanding the stars and their influence on our lives. As I walked into his home, I found his presence intriguing—he was tall and slender, and his aura exuded a mix of ancient wisdom and modern intellect, shaped by his decades of studying Jyotish astrology and his former career as a human resources manager in the federal government.

As I sat before him, spilling my deepest desires, he studied my chart and looked at my hands with an intensity that felt like he was peering into my soul. Then, he revealed what I now refer to as the thirteen-year prophecy. This prophecy was a forecast guiding me toward a destiny beyond what I could imagine for myself. The prophecy also spoke of a man, a soulmate, who would enter my life in my late thirties to early forties. The description of this man was detailed and intriguing—older or mature beyond his years, creative with technical expertise, possibly a foreigner, with a deep affinity for the color blue and a love of music. But the most captivating part of Allen's soulmate prediction was that I would have an injured spouse, a man sporting a unique mark or scar on his lower body that would identify him as my destined partner.

This revelation left me in a state of mixed emotions. Part of me was excited at the prospect of finding true love, but my impatient mind dreaded the long wait.

Thirteen years? For real? Why?

I remember asking the astrologer if there was any possible way to fast forward this fate. Can't I press "skip intro" on the Netflix show of my life, and get to the good stuff already? Allen's answer, as expected, was a blend of wisdom and realism: fate unfolds at its divine pace, and cares not for our earthly haste. As someone who thrives on solving problems, I couldn't accept this. So, I urged Allen for a solution, a way to engage with my destiny head-on. That's when he introduced me to an ancient remedy, a ritual that seemed as old as time. He advised me to feed crows with black food before noon for six consecutive Saturdays. If I missed a Saturday, I had to start over until I had fed crows for six Saturdays in a row, without fail. This task, strange and almost surreal, was meant to clear delays and obstacles from my life and weave my desires into the fabric of the universe.

While I was borderline incredulous, I was also determined to embrace this mystical journey, so I moved forward with the ritual. Every Saturday morning, I would venture out to find crows. I explored parks with tall trees and ventured near ravines and other mysterious corners of the city. My offerings were specific—almonds covered in dark chocolate and pieces of dark rye bread because I felt a little fancy. The ritual was not without its challenges. There were times I struggled to find crows, weeks I forgot to buy the food, or times I got there too late. But with each successful offering, I felt a profound transformation within me. It was as if the crows and I shared a secret understanding, a silent language that transcended spoken words.

This ritual became more than feeding birds; it was a journey of self-discovery and spiritual awakening. The crows, known in many cultures as intelligent beings that help us deeply connect to our creativity and intuition, became my teachers. They taught me the value of patience, discipline, and perseverance. I learned that the true magic lay in the act of doing, in committing oneself to a purpose larger than life. The ritual became a mirror, reflecting the qualities I needed to cultivate within myself to manifest the life I desired.

As years passed, I grew in ways I hadn't imagined, refining myself physically, emotionally, and spiritually like a diamond under pressure. Whenever I felt the need, I did another round of crow-feeding, which reminded me to appreciate the magic in the mundane. Over time, the ritual of feeding crows became a grounding practice, a reminder of the lessons I learned and the destiny I was moving towards. In moments of impatience, confusion, or even despair, the crows brought me back to clarity and purpose. They became symbols of my journey, reminding me of the power of consistency and commitment.

Another transformative moment came years later when I discovered the power of life mapping and creating a vision book from Laura a gifted numerologist and tarot card reader. This tool was an evolution of the vision board concept—a book that became my guide, filled with images, affirmations, and dreams. It was a creative and visual manifestation technique that allowed me to clearly articulate my desires. Every morning and night, I would immerse myself in my vision book to align my energy with my goals. This practice taught me the power of visualization and the importance of keeping my dreams alive in my consciousness every day.

Then, at the age of forty, on a seemingly ordinary evening, my story took a magical turn. After fifteen years of traveling and living in various cities across Canada and internationally, I found myself back in my hometown. Wanting to make new friends and try something new, I decided to take Latin dance classes. Little did I know that this simple decision would lead me to the fulfillment of the thirteen-year prophecy.

In that dance class, I noticed a tall, dark, and hand-some man wearing a Batman T-shirt. As fate would have it, we ended up talking, and eventually, we be-gan dating. With each date, the pieces of the prophe-cy began to fall into place: he revealed his love for the color blue, his upbringing in Africa before immigrat-ing to Canada, his passion for music, and his creative career in graphic design and filmmaking. And then, one day, I saw it—a beautiful scar running down his right leg, the sign Allen had foretold thirteen years ago.

At that moment, everything made sense. The waiting, the feeding of the crows, the vision book—it all led me to this man, the one the universe had chosen for me. It was a profound realization that there are no acci-dents in life, and that the universe had been aligning our paths all along to guide us toward each other in its perfect timing. God is never late, and I now see this to be true. Thirteen years following my fateful astrology session with Allen, and thirteen months after we first met, my wonderful husband and I tied the knot in a joyful ceremony filled with love and laughter. This thirteen-year journey taught me the incredible power of patience, vision, and faith. The crows taught me the importance of perseverance and the magic of committing to the work at hand. The vision book showed me the power of focusing on my desires and aligning my energy with my dreams.

And this man, my husband and soulmate, is the living proof that the universe listens and responds in ways beyond our understanding.

As I share my story with you, I invite you to explore the depths of your heart and soul. Embrace the possibility of magic in your life, nurture the seeds of your dreams, and believe in the power of the universe to bring them to fruition. My journey is a testament to the fact that when we align our energy, our mind, our body, and our spirit with our dreams, we will manifest our deepest desires in perfect timing.

Bio

Christina Bellevue is an author and consultant who assists travelers in thriving mentally, physically, and spiritually while living overseas. After a transformative two-year stay in Japan, Christina is now dedicated to promoting beauty, positivity, travel, and wellness through her writing and her production company, Christina in Colour.

For more information, you can reach her by email at christinaincolour@gmail.com.

Chapter 2

Divine Flow

By Lucille Boettger

Reminder to self: Trust the universe—it knows far more than I do. And what appears to be a block or setback is sometimes a blessing in disguise! A part of me knew this but had forgotten until a sequence of events in 2020 reminded me that there is power and magic in each of us if we can listen to our deep whispers and dare to imagine a new way of being and behaving.

I owned a lovely century home situated on a hill with a beautiful view across the Ottawa River, and there was an empty lot beside me that gave the impression of being in the country instead of the city. It was my oasis and sanctuary from the busyness of life, and I hoped one day to purchase the adjoining lot to expand my peaceful environment and secure my privacy. One day, upon return from a business trip, I saw a *sold* sign on the lot next door, and those hopes were dashed. I had not even known it had been for sale and felt cheated out of an opportunity to make my dreams come true. To add insult to injury, I was soon notified that the new owners were seeking permission from the city to build two multiple-unit dwellings that would not only deprive me of my view and tranquility but add four families as immediate neighbors.

I immediately contacted the city to register my opposition to the building plans, hoping to mitigate the impact of the situation by asking that they refuse the application to permit the construction of more than one home. When the city ruled in favor of allowing multiple dwellings, I continued to fight by registering a formal appeal, hoping to find a way to sway the decision to preserve some of my privacy.

The pandemic emerged amid all this personal turmoil, and like everyone else, my world turned upside down. My old ways of obtaining support and coping weren't available to me, and I scrambled to find new ways of doing things in addition to adapting to a new way of working. Exhaustion and fatigue began to set in. To make matters worse, travel within Canada was restricted, and quarantine requirements and lockdowns prevented me from seeing my grandchildren, who lived far away in Nova Scotia. I felt isolated and overwhelmed, and all the scenarios running through my mind were discouraging. The universe seemed to be conspiring against me.

One night, drained of all hope for a positive resolution, I decided to try to stop the endless chatter running through my mind and see if I could recreate the feeling of inner peace that had previously been my norm. Since I felt powerless to change what was happening outside, I needed to focus on what I could influence—my feelings. In the stillness of a deep meditation, I surrendered control and asked the angels for help.

The next day, I awoke with an epiphany! With remote work now being the norm, I could sell my house, move closer to my grandchildren, and keep my job! Thank you, angels! But doubt soon set in, and the first thought that came to mind was that I didn't have enough free time to get the house ready for being on the market. Moreover, who would want to buy a century-old home with new construction planned on the lot next door? And then it occurred to me. Perhaps the owners of the adjoining lot would be willing to buy me out if I withdrew the appeal that was preventing them from beginning construction on their project! This could be a mutually beneficial agreement that would be easy to implement and seemed like an ideal solution to my problems. A glimmer of hope peeked out from my despondency.

I immediately contacted the owners of the adjoining lot, and much to my delight, discovered that they were interested in my proposition! We agreed to get three separate evaluations and average the results to determine a fair price for my property. They chose one real estate agent, and I contacted two—one of whom had recently left an unsolicited contact card in my mailbox.

After completing the evaluations, two of the agents came back with the same figure, and the third was significantly higher. However, the owners of the adjoining lot determined that even the lowest valuation was out of their price range. Disappointed that my idea had not borne fruit, I now needed to decide whether to list my house for sale and prepare it for showings in a COVID environment. Christmas was coming, and we were in lockdown. After some soul-searching, I advised the real estate agents of my decision to wait until spring to pursue the sale of my home. That night, I resigned myself to waiting another six months before I could hug my grandchildren and mentally prepared to devote all my free time to preparing the house so it would sell quickly once listed.

Little did I know that the universe had other plans for me! The following morning, the agent whose contact card I found in my mailbox called me. He was excited to share that he had secured a no-conditions offer for me for my home. While doing his groceries that morning, he ran into a former client, discussed my property, and as a result, I would be able to sell my house at the highest valuation without having to list my home! I was ecstatic! I quickly accepted the offer and began to search for a new home in Nova Scotia near my grandchildren.

To my dismay, there weren't many properties available in the area at the time. I enlisted my daughter to help view houses that had potential, trusting that something suitable would emerge. After a few disappointing visits, one possibility remained: a lakefront home that had been on the market for some time. What was spectacular about the property was its location and size: a large home on a wooded lot that would allow me to welcome and host my four children for family gatherings. The detractor was that the house interior and yard required a significant amount of attention, which explained why it had not sold previously. While this last house was also unappealing at first, a little voice inside me said to look beyond appearances—and so I did.

After some number crunching, I made an offer to purchase the home for less than the asking price so I could afford the required repairs and renovations. To my delight, the offer was accepted even though the real estate market was starting to soar. I had a new home! I no longer needed to settle for the impression of being in the countryside—I was now going to be surrounded by peace, quiet, and healing nature. Instead of having a view of nature from the top of a hill over houses and streets, I would watch beautiful sunsets with brilliant colors reflecting in the water in front of me. This new home was everything I had dreamed of and more!

By that time, I trusted the universe was orchestrating everything from behind the scenes, and understood that my task was to keep moving in the direction of the flow. If things fell into place easily, I was on the right path. If I was working hard and pushing, a course correction was required. Divine flow came into being! So many synchronicities, or as I prefer to think of them, miracles, occurred during the entire process of this move, each confirming that there was a higher power at work.

Since then, not a day has gone by that I have not remembered that there is a grander plan for me that transcends what seems to be obstacles or setbacks. I cultivate peace within so that peace will be experienced outside. I trust the divine flow that I discovered and trust that the universe will do what it can to support me in making the world a better place.

Bio

Lucille grew up the fourth eldest in a family of nine children on a farm in rural Manitoba. She is the mother of four adult children, and lives in Nova Scotia near three grandsons that she adores! Lucille's mission in life is to bring peace to the world, one person at a time, by helping individuals respect and appreciate themselves and each other. Lucille is privileged to support the development of personal resiliency and peacemaking through her work with various organizations such as the Canadian Armed Forces, the United Nations, CINERGY® conflict coaching, and the Mental Health Commission of Canada.

Contact via Linked In at
linkedin.com/in/lucille-boettger-a8635012

Chapter 3

The Journey of Transformation from Healing to Service

By Crystal Camp-Kravtsov

The world began to crumble, leaving Crystal lost in a sea of contemplation, where she questioned everything she had known, as well as the people in her life. At that crucial juncture, her mentor recommended ten books to aid in her transformation. Ironically, she wasn't an avid reader at the time; in fact, she had a strong aversion to it. However, inspired by an intuitive nudge, she ordered two books from the list: A *New Earth* by Eckhart Tolle and *The Untethered Soul* by Michael A. Singer. Little did she know that the universe was at work, guiding her through several remarkable signs and synchronicities. These two books served as a revelation as if they were meticulously chosen by destiny itself. They showed her that by aligning her thoughts and intentions with a higher, more positive vibration, she could manifest her desired experiences and circumstances. This realization ignited a profound sense of empowerment and deepened the connection to her spiritual self. It was the universe's way of affirming she was on the right path.

The signs and synchronicities began to appear with such remarkable consistency that they couldn't be ignored. They seemed tailor-made for Crystal, repeating themselves until they were impossible to overlook. Angel numbers, those mysterious messengers from the universe, began pouring into her life, their presence as vivid as a sunbeam. Rainbows, like vibrant brushstrokes on the sky's canvas, often graced her with their breathtaking beauty. These magical and transformative moments weren't fleeting; they became a consistent source of joy and wonder, rekindling the playful spirit within her. It was as if the universe was reaching out with a cosmic invitation, urging her to embark on a profound spiritual journey with a heart filled with curiosity and a deepening connection to the spiritual realm. She delved into various spiritual practices. Guided meditations, performed in a tranquil sanctuary of her own making, began to reveal themselves as open channels of pure lightness, akin to stepping into the dreamlike world we all secretly yearn for. This transformational journey was nothing short of encouraging. Guided by patience and practice, she began embarking on 30-minute to 1-hour meditations. Each session left her elated, soaring with confidence in her progress. The universe had opened doors and paved a path she couldn't help but follow.

Crystal's spiritual journey reopened the doors to her psychic abilities, which initially felt both scary and strangely familiar. As she explored these open doors, she began to recollect her childhood memories, re-alizing that she had possessed these gifts since her early years. More and more aspects of her abilities started to feel like old friends as she continued on her spiritual path. During guided meditations like 'Meet your spirit guides,' she noticed a growing clari-ty in her visions when she closed her eyes. The mes-sages she received through inner knowing and hear-ing were abundant. This was the moment when she rekindled her intuitive mediumship skills, a gift she had suppressed since childhood due to fear. Crystal had struggled with fear, but she had found a pow-erful tool to combat it: affirmations. Her favorite, "I am safe," repeated like a calming mantra, helped her overcome the fear associated with her abilities. The daily repetition of affirmations served to reprogram her subconscious mind, aligning her thoughts with her desires. After experiencing trauma, our bodies can remain in a state of fight or flight, falsely signaling danger. Affirmations play a crucial role in reprogramming our minds, reminding us that we are indeed safe, even when past experiences suggest otherwise.

Crystal heeded an inner nudge to start journaling her thoughts, discovering a powerful tool for various aspects of her life. Journaling became an outlet for expressing gratitude, releasing pent-up emotions, addressing those who had hurt her, articulating her intentions and desires, and celebrating her remarkable progress. To this day, she passionately recommends the practice of writing and journaling to her clients, as she knows firsthand the profound difference it can make when you release your thoughts onto the page. As a quick and transformative method, she suggests writing a heartfelt letter to someone, pouring out feelings, expressing gratitude for the lessons learned, and offering forgiveness where it's needed. The final step involves a symbolic act of release. You can burn the letter in a safe container outdoors, if possible, or tear it into pieces, completing the cathartic process. For Crystal, working with the element of fire adds a sense of empowerment to the process, and when combined with writing, it fuels the letting go process, creating space for more positive manifestations. She has delved into numerous healing modalities and therapeutic techniques, including quantum energetic healing and past-life regression hypnosis. Her approach is rooted in the belief that everyone should explore what resonates with them, as not every method is a one-size-fits-all solution. Throughout her journey, each modality she encountered became a valuable tool, leading her to integrate multiple healing approaches. This fusion of techniques has given rise to her unique and authentic approach to healing.

One of the techniques that she wholeheartedly embraces is the use of vision boards. It was one of the first tools she adopted during her awakening, and she even involved her children in this creative process. As a homeschooling mom, she values the nurturing of creativity in both her and her children, fostering their manifesting skills and healing abilities. When she achieves something on her vision board, she doesn't stop there. She revisits her desires and dreams, setting her sights on more significant achievements. Behind each aspiration lies a powerful *why* that fuels her intentions. Crystal firmly believes that by setting clear intentions in this manner, the universe becomes more inclined to assist you. For those who create vision boards, she offers words of encouragement, advising them not to be discouraged if their desires don't manifest immediately. Practice is akin to playing a video game with various levels of achievement. The universe often provides valuable lessons before granting your wishes. What had initially started as a quest for personal growth and material desires had transformed into a path of profound inner transformation and service to others. This deep connection to the universe not only opened doors to personal growth but also inspired a greater purpose: empowering the journey of inner transformation and a commitment to service. It's a reminder that our connection to the universe is not only a source of personal enrichment but also a path toward making a meaningful impact on the lives of others.

Crystal embarked on a transformative journey by enrolling in a mentoring program designed to accelerate her healing process, enrich her healing toolbox, shed limiting beliefs, and explore the depths of emotions and the Akashic records. On this profound healing journey, she confronted the challenge of unlearning conditioned behaviors and thought patterns. This meant questioning her own beliefs and working through triggers, resulting in a bumpy yet emotionally transformative road. The process demanded patience, forgiveness, self-acknowledgment, and letting go, all essential elements of her personal growth. Throughout her exploration of these magical healing processes, she gained a profound understanding of rewiring the brain through neural programming. She emphasizes the importance of persistence, as every practice contributes to forging new neural pathways in the brain. This journey into the energetic field pushed her to step out of her comfort zone, ultimately leading her to become a coach and mentor. Clients have often praised her intuitive guidance and her ability to connect with them on a deep, soulful level. Crystal's spiritual and manifestation journey has continued to evolve in ways she couldn't have foreseen when she first embarked on this path. What began as a quest for personal success has metamorphosed into a profound mission of service dedicated to uplifting and empowering others.

Bio

Crystal is a multifaceted individual, embodying the roles of a D-codes™ practitioner, energetic healer, psychic medium, and QHHT practitioner. With a passionate commitment to personal growth and transformation, she embarked on a journey that unfolded through profound healing experiences, challenging her to shed limiting beliefs and delve into the depths of emotions and Akashic records.

Beyond her spiritual journey, Crystal's life is enriched by her three children, and she embraces the role of a homeschool mom, nurturing creativity and learning in the family. In her free time, you'll find her tending to her garden, immersing herself in the written word, cherishing the company of animals, and basking in the beauty of the great outdoors.

Crystal's life story is a testament to the transformative power of self-discovery and the unwavering commitment to service and upliftment. With a heart open to the universe, she continues to explore the endless possibilities of spiritual growth and healing while also finding joy in the simple pleasures of life.

Thegiftedpsychichealer.com

Chapter 4

Divine Expansion: Part I

By April Chambers

"Expansion within is the journey of self-discovery, personal growth, and the unfolding of one's potential."
—Albert Einstein

"At any moment of the day, some desire is in the process of coming true. Old seeds we planted (perhaps forgotten about) are bringing results, mixed with larger results to come. The point is to make your children aware that the universe (or spirit or God) is always listening; none of us is alone. We are constantly being heeded."
—Deepak Chopra

I love my life at 69, though it hasn't always been this way. Reflecting on the past, I see each memory as a storehouse of valuable lessons and unexpected blessings. Through the years, these memories have gradually molded me, influencing my responses to life's challenges. Some of the toughest lessons required the guidance of a therapist, prayer, meditation, and wisdom from helpful books, transforming them into profound blessings. I embrace life while always aware that I am supported by God, never traversing this journey alone. My alchemy during and after the following account of my experiences underpins all of this. At the young age of 15, I underwent one of the most monumental experiences of my life. It propelled my personal and spiritual growth exponentially while sowing the seeds for my future. The adventure transcended the usual constraints of my existence and caused me to discover more of who I was meant to be.

Fifty-three years ago, my family relocated from California to Pennsylvania due to my stepfather's new job, marking the start of a fresh academic journey for me at a new school. I found myself sitting in the first row, second to the last seat, during my freshman year of high school, facing the difficulties of a challenging home life. I often sat towards the back of the classroom, not wanting to be noticed. I was reserved both at home and at school. As the school year neared its end, I had only forged one friendship on campus.

I sat there in a daze, day after day, as I had done for months, listening to the daily announcements. Then, one day, there was a revelation: "How would you like to get away for the summer?" It was as though the heavens had parted, and angelic voices sang, "This is your chance, April!" I couldn't fathom the purpose of this mysterious message, but the voice on the intercom resonated like divine guidance, instructing me to meet in the library after school.

I followed my inner guidance, prompting me to head to the library. The library rendezvous unveiled an enticing proposition of the possibility of becoming an exchange student. I eagerly snatched the application, unable to contain my excitement, as I rushed home to ask my parents for their approval. To my astonishment, in a mere five minutes, they responded with a resounding "Yes!" It felt like a miraculous moment, and I was overwhelmed with gratitude towards my parents!

Following my interview with the International Fellowship Exchange Student Organization, a mere two weeks later, an acceptance letter arrived. My heart soared with joy at the prospect of a summer adventure. The letter detailed my journey: I would fly to Managua, Nicaragua, and from there, journey with my host family to Ocotal, a quaint village established in 1543, perched on the border of Honduras. For three months, I would become part of their household. For the first time in a long while, optimism washed over me as I clutched that letter, dancing to the tunes of the Beatles, feeling freedom fill my soul. The seeds of change were in the air!

In the warmth of June, I embarked on a solo flight from Pittsburgh to Miami. With guidance from the exchange student representative, I found myself on a small TACA Airlines plane. After enduring four hours of turbulence, including a brief layover in San Salvador and munching on a sandwich from a brown paper bag distributed on the plane, we finally landed in Managua.

Stepping cautiously down the aircraft's stairs onto the wet tarmac, I followed the other passengers into the terminal. The air inside was sweltering, heavy with humidity, yet oddly hushed for an airport. It appeared that only airport staff and those from my flight were permitted within. This was a time void of cell phones; no one awaited my arrival, and my knowledge of Spanish was limited to a few phrases.

Suddenly, a customs agent seized my weathered old Samsonite suitcase and aggressively flipped it open on a metal table in front of me. He meticulously examined each item, and to my mortification, feminine napkins scattered everywhere! Armed soldiers stood sentinel at every exit while curious locals peered through the windows as if we were celebrities. Trembling and fraught with fear, I was a stranger in a land where the autocratic Somoza family held sway. The oppression in the air was palpable, and security tersely handed me back my suitcase, commanding me to reassemble its contents. With tears welling up inside, I complied swiftly! Looking back, I recognize that this moment sparked the seeds of the awakening of my power within to think for myself and further cultivated my resilience.

I collected myself, assessed the situation, and realized that I needed to venture out in the massive crowd peering in through the windows. With my sticker name tag proudly displayed on my chest, I summoned my courage and moved forward. I retrieved a piece of paper from my pocket with the name "Margarita Ramos" written on it. Though I was filled with fear, the thought of going back home was not an option. I wandered for about ten minutes, searching for a woman I had never seen while constantly bumping into people who spoke a language I couldn't understand. In retrospect, this was the seed of faith in me showing up! I was protected!

Miraculously, a tall, imposing woman stopped in front of me, gazed into my eyes, studied my name tag, and then pointed to hers. It was a match with the name on the paper I was clutching! Relief washed over me. She smiled, motioned for me to follow her, and led me to her car, which was already occupied by her four children, ranging from 7 to 17 years old. The journey took about five hours to travel 166 miles on bumpy dirt roads, with occasional stops for animals crossing our path. As I bounced around in their light blue 1960s sedan, the world outside seemed to be painted in lush green hues, with beautiful fields and trees in every direction. In retrospect, the vision of the ride has been a blessing to recall.

During the drive, I couldn't help but let anxious thoughts about where I would be sleeping for the next three months creep into my mind. However, simultaneously, I could feel the warmth and kindness of the family through their glances, smiles, and attempts to communicate with me. Instinctively, I knew this was a loving family, and I would be safe with them. That awareness brought me a sense of peace. Even in this brief moment, the seeds of the knowing that the importance of love and safety are paramount in our lives were present.

Surprisingly, their house resembled the one I had in the United States, with one notable difference: the water that flowed from all the faucets was a disconcerting dark brown. To counter this issue, the maids had placed a horse trough in my bathroom, filled with clean water on the day of my arrival, intended for bathing. However, that same water remained there for about five days! I was reticent to speak in general and lacked the specific Spanish to communicate politely about the now dirty water lingering in the trough. I distinctly recall refraining from taking a shower or bath during those days, instead resorting to scraping the scum that formed on the water's surface and using that water with a touch of soap to wash up. In hindsight, this experience allowed me to further explore resilience and adaptability within!

Continue reading about April's journey in the next article.

Bio

April Chambers is a dedicated educator with over 30 years of experience across all grade levels in public school systems. She earned a Bachelor of Arts in elementary education, majoring in Sociology with a minor in Spanish, and also holds a Master's degree in elementary education and bilingual education. April played a pivotal role in establishing a successful, inclusive multi-age school in Scottsdale, Arizona, and later transitioned to supporting ESL teachers. Beyond her career, she's a devoted wife and mother to three sons and their spouses, and a joyful grand-mother to two granddaughters. In retirement, she continues her passion for learning through oil paint-ing and travel, embracing the opportunities that life offers with gratitude and belief that all is in divine order.

Chapter 5

Divine Expansion: Part II

By April Chambers

"Even when you think you have your life all mapped out, things happen that shape your destiny in ways you might never imagine." —Deepak Chopra

Margarita firmly instructed me to drink only the bottled, filtered water they supplied. However, despite following this advice, my stay concluded with a dismal diagnosis of hepatitis (I was put in the hospital for the last five days of my trip and told to get on the plane and go home). Each day, life's demands necessitated conversations with Margarita. It became evident how crucial it was to acquire a grasp of the Spanish language, prompting me to diligently study my dictionary every night. I longed to converse with my host family and the broader community. Looking back, I realize that learning to speak up for myself in a foreign language was a push and practice for me to speak up for myself in any language! The seed of growing my voice was a part of this moment!

I attended a girls' business school that convened daily in a humble adobe room across the street from my host family's home. Initially, forming friendships was a challenging endeavor due to the language barrier. I vividly recall moments when the girls would chuckle at my attempts to speak in Spanish. One day, while at school, the oppressive humidity caused the heel of my shoe to detach. A student playfully tossed it to another girl, teasing me to chase it. These instances, among others, etched lasting impressions of the emotions one experiences when entering a new group. I unmistakably felt like an outsider, profoundly alone. These emotional imprints were the seeds of providing me with valuable insights into how I could support students in the future as a teacher. I became sensitized to the feelings of those who feel excluded. Throughout these hard moments, I seemed to find the resilience that urged me to persevere each night, memorizing new words. I prayed nightly and had faith that I would find peace.

Upon my return in August of 1970, I learned that Nicaragua ranked as the second poorest country in the Western Hemisphere! This made sense because of the stark poverty I had witnessed in Ocotal. On several occasions, I received invitations to visit the one-room mud-brick homes of some of the girls my age from the business school. It had already become clear to me that my host family was part of a small group of affluent families in the village. I also sensed a certain disconnection from Margarita when I expressed my desire to visit my newfound friend (from a low socioeconomic neighborhood), but she allowed me to go nevertheless. The simple one-room homes often had animals tethered to them and seemed to go on forever! The family I visited was extremely kind and offered me some cookies from a cookie tin. Encounters like these served as poignant reminders of the profound economic disparities in the community. The girls I befriended at the school were a delight to be around and invited me to be on the school float in a town parade. They assisted me in finding a traditional Nicaraguan dress to look like them! This memory offered deep insight into universal connections, love and community, a true blessing in hindsight.

My personal growth continued to flourish as I immersed myself in their vibrant culture. I was honored to participate in a Quinceanera Ceremony, a celebration marking a 15-year-old girl's transition into adulthood, for a family friend named Martha.

A talented local seamstress meticulously crafted a stunning peach dress, while a small beauty salon artfully arranged intricate bun curls for me. I strolled down the aisle with a dashing escort named Salvador and shared his company at the reception. The entire experience drew striking parallels to the weddings I had attended back home. I was gifted a charming little notebook where young men would ask for dances. That evening, I danced all night! It was an unforgettable, joy-filled evening, a true blessing that left an indelible mark on my heart. This experience was the specific seed of an experience that showed up decades later in my life. As a self-contained middle school teacher, I first hand understood the importance of this ceremony when I heard that one of my students, turning 15, could not afford to have a Quinceanera. Our class collaborated to craft a stunning Quinceanera, capturing the local newspaper's attention! The understanding gained from these cultural insights supported numerous newcomers who went through my classrooms.

Another experience that was different from all others and was particularly distressing involved observing a ceremony in which around 20 chickens were dangled upside down from a clothesline. Their feet were tightly bound to the line, filling the air with shrill cries. I was utterly shocked. Then, I witnessed a man on horseback, breaking away from a group of horsemen, charge toward a selected chicken and wrench its neck in an attempt to detach it. The scene was a gory spectacle, resembling a horror movie. Perplexed, I inquired about the purpose of this act, and someone explained that it was an ancient belief among ranchers that if they could decapitate a chicken in this manner, it would bring prosperity to their crops. He further clarified that when the Catholic Church integrated into the community, they urged the people to abandon certain traditions but permitted them to keep a few so they would embrace the church. The challenging moment cultivated the awareness that everyone views life uniquely. More than fifty years later, I've learned that staying curious instead of passing judgment is a powerful tool for refraining from making judgments about others.

The countless experiences from this immersion experience in this foreign culture are too many to mention here, but I am grateful beyond words for the seeds that have flourished in me from this experience over more than five decades that have followed. I departed Nicaragua with a multitude of lessons and blessings that have profoundly transformed me. Of course, I have years of other life experiences that have fertilized these seeds, as well. Eckhart Tolle's words capture life so well, "Life will give you whatever experience is most helpful for the evolution of your consciousness. How do you know this is the experience you need? Because it is the experience you are having at the moment." I can trace the following aspects of my transformation to the seeds of my experiences in Nicaragua that summer:

Mastering the Spanish language

Fostering an open-minded appreciation of humanity

Recognizing love transcends all boundaries

Knowing that inner strength and resilience are in me

Understanding the privilege of the home I have in the US

Embracing the truth that we are all equal, regardless of our differences

Knowing my voice matters

Knowing my purpose to help second language learners and marginalized students

I remain strong in the awareness of the divine's love and support for me

Knowing I am worthy

Knowing I created my dream

About eight years later, when I decided to become a teacher, the imprint from this experience created a bonfire within me to help second language learners and marginalized students. This purpose inspired me afresh each morning for thirty years to have a burning desire to help over five hundred students realize their strength and power while guiding them on their journeys.

Looking back on this snapshot of my memories from a powerful experience, even though it was difficult at times, I see how it increased the quality of my life and facilitated my helping so many students from ages 5 to 17. It is interesting to observe that because I didn't want to be at home that summer, I was catapulted into choosing to become an exchange student, which sowed countless personal growth opportunities! It is clear how all the events in my life are connected, and this awareness has increased my faith in today and the days that lie ahead! I know I am divinely guided and loved, transformed daily through the alchemy of the experiences in my life, turning challenges into golden opportunities, always. I eagerly anticipate the insights that each day brings!

Bio

April Chambers is a dedicated educator with over 30 years of experience across all grade levels in public school systems. She earned a Bachelor of Arts in elementary education, majoring in Sociology with a minor in Spanish, and also holds a Master's degree in elementary education and bilingual education. April played a pivotal role in establishing a successful, inclusive multi-age school in Scottsdale, Arizona, and later transitioned to supporting ESL teachers. Beyond her career, she's a devoted wife and mother to three sons and their spouses, and a joyful grandmother to two granddaughters. In retirement, she continues her passion for learning through oil painting and travel, embracing the opportunities that life offers with gratitude and belief that all is in divine order.

Chapter 6

Don't Let This Happen to You

By Stacy Christopher

I grew up in the Sixties, watching "I Love Lucy" reruns daily. In one episode, Lucy decides to become a writer. With a nod to Tennessee Williams, she calls herself "Rhode Island Red" and writes her autobiography. After submitting her manuscript for publication, she receives a call informing her that a chapter of her book will be featured in a "how to" book for aspiring writers. She's overjoyed until she learns that her chapter will be a cautionary one, entitled "Don't Let This Happen to You." In that spirit, please allow me to share my manifestation mishap.

I first encountered the concept of manifestation at a Church of Religious Science. I had defected from a mainstream congregation that had become less inclusive, and no longer felt like a spiritual home.

Finding a new church seemed daunting, not nearly as simple as asking where someone gets their hair cut. I sat down with the phone book and started calling the Dial-A-Prayer numbers of every church that offered one. I decided that I would keep listening to messages until I heard one that was inclusive, non-dogmatic, and, most of all, reasonable-sounding. After a long day of crossing out listings that didn't resonate, I finally found one that did.

Religious Science/Science of Mind is a New Thought based on the writings of Ernest Holmes. (Currently, the meeting places are called Centers for Spiritual Living.) In his study of major world religions, Holmes noticed that they had commonalities despite their differences. He took these shared concepts and built a philosophy around them. One of the basic tenets is cause and effect. We are constantly creating our own realities with our words, thoughts and actions. To illustrate the constructive use of this power, he outlined a five-step process (Recognition, Unification, Realization, Thanksgiving and Release) called Spiritual Mind Treatment.

The steps are a way for us to remember who we are and why we are here. When we feel out of balance, it's a way to realign. We recognize that there is a Presence (called God, Spirit, Higher Power or whatever feels right for you) in and through all things, including ourselves, and that Its very nature is creativity. We consciously unify with It. It is love, joy, harmony, prosperity and so much more, and so are we. We realize that those circumstances we desire already exist in potential, and we call them forth into form. We give thanks, and confidently release our declaration to the universe to manifest in the perfect way and at the perfect time.

The first letters of the steps are RURTR, or "R U Ready To Receive?" The Children's Church version is "God is, I am, I want, thank you, goodbye." I've oversimplified, but those were the basics I learned. Our thoughts and words have power. We can spiritually manifest our intentions, and we are responsible for doing the physical, mental and emotional work to prepare for their arrival. For example, before bringing home a puppy, we would puppy-proof the house and buy toys, beds, food and pee pads. We might read up on how to be good puppy parents or sign up for training classes. We would work on being ready to both receive the blessing and be good stewards of it.

With that in mind, let's circle back to our girl Lucy/Rhode Island Red and her "Don't Let This Happen to You" chapter. I have my own chapter like that. Allow me to tell the story of how it all went very wrong when I tried to circumvent the co-creative force. Hi, my name is Stacy, and I did it this way, so you don't have to.

Around the year 2000, I'd been in several relationships that were less than ideal. The common thread in those relationships was me, but I didn't choose to look at that or to do the necessary work to make myself the sort of person who would attract a suitable partner and maintain a healthy relationship. Instead, I set out to put the "man" in manifestation, so to speak. I had my eye on two men and left it to the universe to do an immediate cosmic coin flip and decide which was the one for me. (Spoiler alert: neither was the one for me.) I delusionally approached the universe like an optometrist, asking, "Which looks better, A or B?"

I threw myself into the "Man-ifestation" process wholeheartedly. I recited affirmations throughout the day. I visualized myself involved with either A or B and occasionally both when I felt greedy. I did what seemed the appropriate prep work on my end, which involved (as is often the case when shallowness prevails) endless sit-ups, new underwear, and resolute hair removal. I placed myself in their lines of vision when I was looking my best. I even bought pink roses and scattered the petals in my bath water while listening to romantic music at the suggestion of a cash-only boardwalk psychic. I was, I thought, ready for the universe to do its thing.

And it did. The universe said, "Okay, friend, as you wish." Sure enough, I found myself in a relationship with one of the men. There was all the intensity and passion I'd imagined, but it quickly flared into destructive chaos. Have you ever seen one of those nature documentaries where two rams run full tilt at one another, brutally crashing their horns together? If you can imagine that happening over and over in an endless loop, you'll have an idea of the relationship's progression. We brought out the absolute worst in each other and in ourselves, with everyone around us as collateral damage. It dragged on and on, long past the point of exhaustion, feeling like sleep paralysis or the quicksand pits in childhood cartoons.

That's what I manifested, so allow me to share what I learned so you "don't let this happen to you." First off, I thought that I knew better than the universe did. I limited its potential to manifest by insisting on either "A" or "B." Had I opened my awareness to include "or something better," the outcome could have been much more beneficial.

I violated the boundary of someone else's free will. In my own mind, I suppose I thought that I would be a good thing for someone, but as it turned out, not so much. I didn't want to see that then, and I forced myself on someone. Consent is a huge part of my spiritual work now; I always ask permission to feel into someone's energy, even if they have specifically asked for a reading. I won't do "relationship readings" unless everyone involved is present. Don't ask me if someone is thinking of you or how they feel about you—ask them. And take the time to think about what you are bringing to the table. I didn't do any of that.

I negatively impacted my friends and family (and his) with my selfish, short-sighted manipulation of the laws of the universe. Again, I clearly thought I would be a real boon to any situation, and, again, not so much. If I had sought to manifest for the highest good of all concerned, the outcome would have been drastically different. I didn't choose to see that at the time.

My hope, friend, is that my missteps will serve as your stepping stones. You can absolutely manifest your desires. After all, you are a microcosm of the universe in physical form, and it is the nature of the universe to create. You are always creating. With every thought, word and action, you create. As Gandhi said, "Be the change you want to see in the world." Pray for a good harvest, but keep using those gardening tools. In Spanish, the proverb is "A Dios rogando, y con el mazo dando:" praying to God and pounding the hammer.

Trust the universe to co-create that which you seek, in the way that will bring the best results, and work on becoming the person who will nurture the blessing received. Embody the characteristics of what you want to manifest. Be open to more, and allow it to manifest in due time, not on your schedule. Seek the highest good for all concerned, that we may all rise up together. You are absolutely amazing, and I wish you all the very best (or something even better)!

Bio

Stacy Christopher (she/her) is an ordained minister, Reiki Master and licensed therapist. It has been her absolute honor to study with the Rev. Dr. Michael Beckwith, globally beloved psychic medium Tony Stockwell, "Psychic Sergeant" Peter Close, renowned animal communicator Elizabeth Ayer Lee, and award-winning podcast creator Ann Theato. Stacy loves working with open-minded creatives on their journey to increase motivation and direction via aligning with their inner guidance. Her passions include advocating for justice and equality, volunteering in animal rescue and being a huge theater nerd.

Website: TheBloomingMystic.com;
FB/IG: The Blooming Mystic.

Chapter 7

The Game of Life

By Becky Cohen

We are all souls having a human experience. I believe this is the very first a-ha moment that occurs in some way, shape or form to all human beings when they go through a spiritual awakening. To awaken the incredible magic within that's waiting to be unleashed, we first must remember who we truly are.

I will never forget the day when I had this incredible revelation. It was 1987 in Australia, around seven years of age. Coming from a traditional Jewish home, and although we weren't religious, we were very insulated. We went to a Jewish school and only knew of our religion. I continuously struggled with the indoctrinated belief system that was passed down. I found it hard to pray to an all-mighty God who sat in the heavens with his grey beard, constantly peering down on us from his almighty throne to ensure we obeyed his commands. I knew deep down that we had it all wrong; however, with no access to spiritually-minded teachers, mentors, or guides, I grew tired of questioning and searching for an alternative response.

Every weekend, my parents would get together with their closest friends. There was always a house full of kids of all ages who hung out together. On this particular Sunday, we played a board game called "The Game of Life."It takes the player from college to retirement, going through life events such as choosing a career, getting married (which was a mandatory step,) buying a house, and having children. The game ends when all players retire, and the person with the most money is declared the winner. We had played this game countless times, but on this particular day, I remember thinking, why is this game designed so that you can't continue until you get married? In that moment, I had an incredible vision! I saw the ceiling above us open up, and just like all of us were staring down at the board game, controlling the pawn's every move as we rolled the dice, I saw several faces in a circle peering down at us like we were the pawns on the board of the game of life! At that time, I couldn't quite grasp what was happening, who they were, or if they were the ones rolling the dice. But either way, I knew we were part of something greater, a grand design, and this game of life we were living was merely a tiny particle that fed into a grander ecosystem. That was the moment a portal opened up for me to explore my connection with the universe.

From that point onward, I became that slightly weird kid. I was obsessed with all things spiritual; I began asking everyone (including strangers) if they believed in reincarnation, and I was manifesting before knowing how it worked. I had always believed I was destined for greatness, but I had no desire to study, to do things the conventional way, or to settle down. I always dreamed of seeing the world and counted down the days till high school ended. I didn't know how it would happen, but I knew I could make it happen and poof, so it was!

I had traveled and lived abroad for quite a few years and saw half the world before returning. My parents were disappointed that I dropped out of university, but deep down, I knew I could make it without a degree. I decided to manifest the easiest way to make some serious cash without a degree and poof again, so it was!

From the outside world looking in, it seemed like I had it all. I somehow made it as a corporate high-flyer, earning six figures from a young age. I had work when I desired to work. I had the convertible, multiple properties, traveled to over fifty countries, and partied like a rockstar. But all of this was to compensate for my soul slowly wilting. For fifteen years, I woke up wishing every workday was Friday, and by Sunday night, I was dreading Monday. I had experienced the most toxic environments and seen the most inhumane acts of harassment, bullying, and unethical business practices that went against every value in my system. I had learned the hard way not to be myself, not to stand out or challenge the status quo. I learned to play the corporate game. Gradually, I lost my voice, my self-expression, and everything that made me, well, me! Most people are trying to manifest financial rewards to feel worthy or valued. In my case, manifesting financial rewards was the price I paid to not feel valued as a human being. I was yearning to find my purpose, my tribe, to make an impact. For someone who was spiritually awake at a young age, I didn't realize how asleep I had become. I had gone into complete (spiritual) burnout. I had to hit rock bottom to hear my inner voice. "It's not your time yet. You need to go and work on *you*," and so I did!

The journey inward took me to the deepest parts of my core. I had to shine a light on my shadow self, the part that became a slave to the system, my lack of self-worth and my value. My identity become wrapped around seeking other's approval and living up to their expectations to belong, to feel accepted.

Nicola Tesla once said, "*If you want to find the secrets of the universe, think in terms of energy, frequency and vibration.*" Energy is the language of our universe. Everything in our universe holds a vibration. The universe is vibrating; we are vibrating. Our feelings are the frequency of vibration, which communicates back into a greater intelligence, the universe.

There was the first revelation. If I was seeking connection, belonging, and purpose, I wasn't ever going to manifest it when I had become so disconnected from my authentic self. My external reality was mirroring my internal reality. We are constantly looking out to the vastness of the cosmos to bring us what we desire, but in order to co-create with the universe, we need to connect with the power from within. This is where your universe lies! Your universe is *you-in-versed!*

The real game-changer was when I discovered Human Design. It is like having a blueprint to your soul, an operating manual on how to find your purpose and alignment. Since we're so unique, it made much more sense that we should be tuning into our unique energetic frequency and vibration!

As I went down the rabbit hole of Human Design, I learned my "*signature*" frequency code when in alignment is satisfaction. I am designed to create a working life I love! To assist us in aligning with our signature; we are gifted with an inner guide, a unique energetic superpower which is called our *"inner authority."* My inner guidance comes from my sacral. I know when I'm making aligned decisions by an instant magnetic pull within my gut, it either lights up with a hell yes or repels with a hell no! When in alignment, I am vibrating out to the universe what lights my soul on fire! I feel alive and become a super attractor to all things satisfying! When out of alignment, I feel my life force slowly diminishing, and when I don't heed the warnings, I will burn out.

As I came back into alignment, I realized I had to go through the pain of my journey to know what my purpose was; otherwise, I wouldn't know the formula to help others do the same. All that I am and all that I have been through is my calling and my mission.

I'm here to help other souls discover their mission, to help those who are stuck on the hamster wheel begging to get off. I'm here to help those souls who know they are destined for greatness, who want to have more impact, and who are calling in to be unapologetically self-expressed. I'm here to awaken and unite as many like-minded souls as I can so we can pioneer a new way of doing business ethically, morally, and humanely. I'm here to ensure we become the majority, and the lower vibrational businesses will have to either evolve or perish! I am here to start a conscious revolution, and poof! So it is!

Bio

Becky Cohen was born in Sydney, Australia. She is the visionary founder of The Conscious Revolution. Becky's a seasoned transformational coach, intuitive, a Business Mentor, and a beacon of conscious leadership. Specializing in Human Design, Becky empowers entrepreneurs to align their businesses with cosmic energies, fostering success with authenticity. With a passion for guiding individuals through profound transformations, she weaves intuitive insights into her coaching, creating a unique blend of wisdom and strategy. Becky is not just a coach; she's a catalyst for conscious evolution, shaping a new paradigm where businesses thrive in harmony with the individual's true design. becky@theconsciousrevolution.com.au

Chapter 8

Blending With Divinity

By Donna Cristal

S pirit inspired me, as I unveil this chapter of my mystical journeys. I hope that this information will help expand awareness of your potential. With pure intentions, I seek to unravel the tapestry of possibilities and the miraculous life each has chosen. Coincidences and synchronicities are the universe speaking to us. In these experiences, the wisdom of self-discovery unfolds.

Exploring Brazil has consistently transformed my perspectives. In October 2011 after attending a presentation about a healer located in Brazil, it sparked my interest. The idea of making a trip to Brazil would not leave me alone. I kept hearing a voice say, "Just take a chance," over and over again. Finally, I made a decision and started preparation for the trip in

January 2012. Everything fell into place. Like it was prearranged, and it was my destiny. Including someone to care for my dog "Lady." This was a genuine concern, given that Lady had undergone emergency surgery two weeks before my departure.

Overflowing with excitement, I'm thrilled to journey to this healing center, this place of miraculous healing. The center is located in a quaint small village of Abadiania in the state of Goias. The most commonly used phrase there is "For those who believe no words are necessary; for those who do not believe, no amount of words are sufficient." During my initial visit, I wanted physical proof for my mind to have full acceptance. By the end of the trip, I was mesmerized by things I could not explain. Every visit is as amazing as the last. This holistic center can assist with illness, physical disorders, relationships, addiction, financial issues, etc.

Despite numerous visits to the center, there has always been this compelling urge to return. Each time has been a transformational experience. It's the incredible energy that draws you. Even through lucid dream states, I have been nudged to return. Sharing pictures of family and friends for healing is one testament. For some, they have felt the energy from Brazil. Witnessing and listening to many miraculous healing stories, including my own, added layers of wonder. I engage in hours-long meditation sessions, experiencing currents of energy flowing through my body, and deepening my connection with spirit. In my experience, the manifesting here is just a commonplace occurrence.

Reflecting on past events, it was the year 2007. I had this yearning to travel to Egypt, so I applied for my passport for the first time. Then, life happened, and I was unable to make the trip, but it remained in my heart. Fast forward to June 2012, and I traveled back to Brazil for another trip. One of the women joining the group arrived during the second week from London. One morning, this woman and I went for coffee, and she announced that she had plans for me to go to Egypt. I was stunned by her comment. I asked her what she meant by that. She reveals that she wants me to facilitate her upcoming group in Egypt for November 2012. I asked her, "What city?" She responds, "Luxor." I had always envisioned I'd be traveling to Cairo, but I didn't resist it and went with the flow. The most remarkable aspect was that the only requirement for me was to purchase my airfare to travel there. This travel opportunity was about to fulfill a longstanding desire.

In November 2012, we arrived in Egypt. We spent the next four days visiting temples. Embarked on a camel ride, and enjoyed sailing on the Nile. There was an interesting encounter with one of the other women on the trip. She approached me, saying, "Don't you remember me?" She believed she recognized me from one of her classes in London. I told her that wasn't possible since I lived in the US. A couple of days later, she again approached me, claiming she knew now that she met me in Brazil. Curiously, I smiled and asked when she had been there. She exclaimed, "January this year." Upon further questioning, she revealed her departure date was January 9th. We had missed each other by 4 days. My arrival date was on January 13th. After determining we were not in Brazil at the same time. She then replies, "That's really weird." I, too, agreed. This was bigger than both of us and had something to do with Brazil. After finishing our business in Luxor that week, we had a few days of free time. We booked a balloon flight to cross over the Valley of the Kings. This was a picturesque viewpoint. We also booked a flight to Cairo for a day trip. I was invited by some of the participants to join them. We visited the Pyramids and an Egyptian museum, and after a long day, we headed back to the airport. After visiting Cairo, I realized that this trip had been more than the perfect outcome. It was better than I could have imagined. Egypt is captivating with its culture, energy, and the allure of its interesting bazaars.

We are universal life force, individually exploring our internal mind. The old keys will not unlock new doors. Our soul's alignment with the divine is the mysterious nature that calls us. Whether you are single, married, or in a partnership, a divine union is the path to wholeness. Achieving balance requires the harmonious integration of both female and masculine energies. Genuine commitment to oneself, or as a couple, a sacred union has that power that thrives and cultivates trust. Deepening this connection involves effective communication and collaborative efforts of co-creating together. Honoring and elevating your relationship with an understanding between you takes being deeply in tune with yourself and or your partner. There's a state of being and frequency to this union. Sexual energy is sacred and an alignment with divinity. You are creating from love, with love, and as love itself. Sacred sexuality is one of the most powerful pathways to divine potential. Merging with the divine has an orgasmic energy, a state of bliss.

Over centuries and eons of time, sexual distortions have been shaping the perceptions and dynamics of the world. This abuse has caused emotional pain and suffering to sever the connection with higher realms. Our human DNA was tampered with through this parasite process. Many are navigating this lifetime in a state of sleepwalking, missing the keys to awakening true potential. Reclaiming our divinity is the rightful aspect of our birthright and involves a journey of self-discovery.

Sharing the following insights stems directly from my experiences. As extensions of our Creator, we embody diverse personalities, each having the same potential within. Raising our frequency starts with meditation. Daily meditation is a powerful tool that contributes to inspiration and balances the nervous system. Beyond that, it enhances mental clarity and deepens intuition. Be mindful, for words and thoughts carry tangible weight; they shape the reality you create. Letting go of negative emotions is a powerful step towards releasing the victim's mindset. Figuring out yourself is time well spent. Your consciousness absorbs everything. Heal the emotional traumas in your life. Integrating the inner child is a crucial aspect. What are the thoughts and feelings that hold you back? Recall what age you were the first time you had the experience. Bring forth this awareness and address the past situations to resolve. This aids in understanding the reasons behind the blockage. These events must unfold for the fragmented parts to be discovered, leading to a more comprehensive understanding and healing.

Shifting your mindset can alter outcomes; releasing what doesn't serve you is a powerful step toward change. Establishing boundaries for yourself is crucial; don't let your fear dictate the path. Acknowledging that the ego may not be a friend, a suggestion of stepping forward with humility to navigate balance. Consider judgment as a projection, possibly an illusion. Reserve judgment unless it aligns with the truth of your personal experience. Patterns often arise from environmental circumstances, shaping perspectives and responses to the world around us. Social consciousness has influenced the impact of societal norms on collective behavior. This key factor will help expand one's understanding beyond surface narratives.

Believe in yourself through loving yourself. Its force will be liberating. Ask yourself what makes you come alive, and go do that. Authenticity shines when expressing your true self. Find your joy through creativity. Unveil the inner genius with the mysterious unknown. Embrace the present, cherish love, and find laughter. Blessings to your journey.

Bio

Donna Cristal is the founder of Divine Destiny LLC. Her passion for travel and the healing arts has guided her to many destinations globally, pursuing the exploration of the spiritual and sacred aspects of these places. These journeys assist with opening the heart and expanding conscious awareness. Her pursuit involves unraveling the mysteries of the unknown through knowledge and truth. She follows this heart-felt journey as a messenger, artist, clairvoyant with intuitive gifts, and a Reiki master. Only *love* bears witness to the power of God.

Contact info: onedivinedestiny@gmail.com

Chapter 9

Unleashed Souls: A Spiritual Unveiling Through Canine Connections

By Danielle Darowz

I guess much of this journey has come full circle most profoundly. A way that as you are on the journey, you might not realize, though, if you have an awareness, you cannot help but see the signs. The signs are waving, jumping, dancing, and hollering for you to see, and boy, will you see them when your eyes are wide open, as is your mind. The images, the feelings, and the sensations flood in right through me.

Let me take you back about twenty years. Yes, I said twenty years. I don't feel that refined, but time has come and gone on this journey. The little lines under my eyes might be an indicator of the knowledge and intuition gathered over the years. Picture a big, beautiful box with pastel watercolors on the outside and inside it is glowing with flecks of gold and a warmth that brings a smile and delight to the memories and signs that have been collected. Some of these are sad memories that I am still in the process of healing, and then there are warmth, love, and splendid memories packed in around it. Those are the signs that keep moving me forward on this journey. This is my life, the journey I have been on. Maybe it is a roller coaster, a wild ride of sorts, but now that I have a complete awareness, it all makes sense. If you love pets, especially dogs, stay with me.

The bond between humans and their pets is sacred. It is a bond unlike any I have ever experienced. The dogs that have come into my life changed me in ways that have profoundly made me who I am today. Being an empath, I feel what they feel. In the beginning, I did not understand what that was, but I felt it. I felt the sadness, and I could hear their thoughts and see images, some of which were difficult to see, too. What was I supposed to do with all of this? How was I supposed to be processing this? What the heck was this?

Some say everything happens for a reason, and some believe in fate. I now believe in all the above, destiny, and the signs from the universe that took me on this journey of awakening. The magic that occurred formed an unbelievable bond and transformed me into the spiritual person I am today.

It was a normal Friday night, snuggled with my big, lovable mutt on the sage-colored couch with subtle floral embroidery, the cushions hugging me as I was winding down after a long week at work. Then, all of a sudden, my body turned, and my eyes met the television, and I could not move. The universe poked me, paused all the time, and made me focus. There it was, a rescue of twenty-three English Setters. Some were being carried over shoulders up a muddy hill, filthy in their bodily fluids, and the faces of the res-cuers were determined and shocked at the same time. These poor darlings were left in an outdoor kennel in inches of their excrement without food or water. Sleeping and sitting up in a corner because they were in fear. Some were so weak they were bare-ly alive. I was frozen. I felt a magnetic pull from the cushions through the television to being transported there with the people. My intuition was firing on full throttle. What was this I was feeling? This moment changed my adult life path.

In the most synchronistic way, miles from my home, this is where a dog I met growing up that my sister dog sat came from. He was a quirky, elusive dog. I did not know about this town or breed prior. However, this day was the first day of the rest of Simon's life and quite possibly the first of the spiritual path the universe was leading me on.

The empath in me felt everything through the news footage. I felt shortness of breath, my chest was tight, and jitters. What was this? This was what has always been there as a child that I tucked away. So many of us who serve others spiritually have had this happen to us as we grew up. It more than likely happens to you, too. I was tuning in and did not understand what it was. Now, I understand the senses of seeing, hearing, feeling, smelling, and tasting. Most importantly, I now thank my guides and how to protect myself with a glass cube technique. Before and during this time, I had no words for what this was or that I was connecting with the universe and animals at a level of sacredness.

The next morning, I called the shelter to donate. I could hear and feel the urgency in the voice that answered the phone. They had never been through something like this before in this tiny country town. All of a sudden, she poured her heart out on the call to me. Does this happen to you in the most random places? This happens to me all the time. This is a sign that you are in a safe place. How beautiful is that to be trusted and make someone feel better and ease their grief? As a psychic medium, easing someone's grief and giving them a hug from heart source is nothing less than amazing and a gift from our spirit guides.

Hours later, I felt a tug, voices that I call drop-ins telling me to go there. I called my best friend, a dog lover too, and told her about this. No questions asked, there we were in my car, driving to a town I had never been to before, which happened to be on my childhood dog's birthday. With a map in her hand, there we were, two young adults headed to an unfamiliar town on long country roads and the crisp smell of the outdoors coming in the car. We were looking at each other, giggling because none of this was planned, hoping we were not about to get lost. It is always an adventure with me. Life takes me to where I need to go in that moment.

We made it to this white-sided rural shelter, set back off the road and pulled into the gravel driveway. We were not alone; many others were drawn to this location to help, too. There was an instant bond between humans who cared and were determined to change the path of these dogs. Dogs were in kennels everywhere, inside and outside. Some kennels had multiple dogs. Volunteers were running on fumes with no sleep, tending to each dog and bathing them to the best of their ability.

I walked inside and met the loveliest lady to hand in a donation. I walked around and went outside to see the dogs there. What happened next was time stopped, and the sun came down on this one kennel, and my spirit guides led me to number four. I dug deep inside and asked for comfort and protection. People were coming from this one kennel and were discussing how this one dog was so shut down he would not even lift his white and black speckled head with his feathered ears and his tail between his legs. He was all alone, shaking uncontrollably on gravel with some food and water. He dropped on all fours when they entered his kennel. I went in and saw the pain in his eyes. I then opened the door to the new love of my life. Slowly, I walked in, and I sat on the ground in silence. I began speaking to him through thoughts, which I later realized was telepathic communication. He sat there looking at me, tilting his head. All of a sudden, he stood up and looked at me as I told him it was going to be okay, as he let me pet him. Others were watching this and could not believe their eyes. Others gravitated toward this kennel to watch the universe in action, and tears began to roll down many faces, including mine. This was a special moment, the beginning of Simon's new life, and my spiritual path that led me to this moment today.

Bio

Danielle Darowz, internationally certified spiritual advisor, psychic medium, and animal intuitive, is navigating a shift from a distinguished two-decade career in information technology to answer her spiritual calling. With a profound connection to animals, she co-founded animal rescue nonprofits, using her spiritual gifts to aid those in need. Danielle's journey seamlessly merges the spiritual and technological realms, offering healing and guidance to both humans and their cherished pets. Embracing a newfound spiritual path, she serves as a beacon of compassion, utilizing her intuitive abilities to connect souls, provide solace, and cultivate a harmonious balance between the earthly and metaphysical dimensions. For more, visit www.danielledarowz.com or follow her on Instagram @danielledarowz.

Chapter 10

Manifesting Despite Myself

By Karen Gabler

I graduated from law school in 1992 and began a 32-year career as an attorney. By 2015, I thought I'd reached a significant peak in my professional path. After years of life as an associate in various law firms, I finally launched my own law firm with a business partner. Three years later, we had expanded our client base by more than 400% and added eight more employees to our team. I was firmly established in the proverbial corner office with a garden view, custom-built desk, and elegant sofa. By all corporate standards, I'd clearly "made it."

I worked around the clock, energized by the idea of building something that was "mine." I was devoted to my team and committed to their growth. I spent my days on management duties and then took my client work home with me to catch up. My business was thriving, but my health deteriorated, I had to make regular apologies to my family, promising to have more time for them when my business obligations settled down. And yet, the business continued to grow. As I worked late each night, I reminded myself that everything I'd been working for was finally paying off.

That summer, I finally agreed to take a short but much-needed vacation with my husband and daughter. As we traveled throughout the Pacific Northwest, we marveled at the stunning landscape. I breathed in the scent of pine wafting from the majestic trees and watched the thundering waves crash along the coastline. We daydreamed about how wonderful it would be to live on the Oregon coast, and I caught my breath as my husband suggested that we consider investing in land where we could build our "forever home."

My excitement grew as I contemplated a peaceful life filled with walks on the beach and hiking in the woods with my family. What would it be like to escape to this coastal haven, leaving everything behind? My soul stirred as my heart fluttered with joy. Almost as quickly, though, I remembered the business I'd worked so hard to build and the commitment I'd made to my team. I couldn't fathom the idea of throwing away everything I'd created. Who would ensure that my law firm continued to thrive, and my legacy remained intact? Who would support and guide my team? How could I leave my loyal clients? I silenced the voice stirring inside me and told my husband that as much as I loved the remarkable ocean views and tree-lined mountains in Oregon, I didn't think I could leave our home in California. I sighed with regret and ignored my sense of loss as I asserted that we would have to consider retirement locations closer to home.

Two months later, my glorious coastal vacation was a distant memory. I returned to the pressure-cooker of business management, doing my best to divide my time between serving my clients and running my law office. During an onslaught of new work and with significant decisions on the table regarding our office footprint, potential new hires, financial decisions and expanding business offerings, I found myself in deep disagreement with my law partner regarding the firm's future. As our debate escalated, I was shocked to discover that we were no longer on the same page. After several acrimonious battles, he abruptly decided to end our partnership, bought me out of the business and assumed sole responsibility for the office lease, business equipment and employment of our team. I wasn't ready to stop working completely and had no desire to start over again, so I negotiated a deal to continue working as a contractor in what was now my former partner's law firm and nursed my wounds.

To my surprise, over time, I slowly began to realize the full extent of the freedom my former law partner inadvertently handed to me in connection with his unexpected dismantling of what I had thought would be my professional legacy. With no ownership in the business, I had no investment to protect and no bills to pay. With no employees of my own, I had no team to mentor. I could continue my own legal work for my clients for as long as I wished, but also could go anywhere I wanted to go and pursue anything I wanted to do without letting anyone down. Having given up my administrative business duties, my time became my own again. I reconnected with my family and volunteered at my daughter's school. I learned to cook and stopped checking my email during dinner. My intuitive gifts expanded and my psychic medium work, once an occasional hobby, became my greatest passion. Feeling devoted to serving others, my spiritual career began to take shape.

Two years later, my husband and I took another vacation to the Oregon coast. As we held hands and breathed in the cool ocean breeze, I thought about the fact that when my former partner ended our joint enterprise, he unknowingly handed me the keys to my golden handcuffs. I no longer felt compelled to remain in California merely to protect my law firm. I no longer felt beholden to my law partner, my team, or my firm. I had been a captain willing to go down with her ship, but instead had been offered a lifeboat. I watched the waves roll onto the shore, smiled at my husband, and said, "Let's retire here!"

We found a wild and beautiful plot of Oregon land located a mile from the beach. Dreaming of a future nestled among the trees, we began designing our forever home and found a builder to launch the project. I set up a countdown clock and we celebrated the declining numbers as we inched closer to our dreams. I announced an official retirement date at my law practice and updated my spiritual website with my expanded intuitive work. I traveled to Oregon to check on the progress of our dream home, breathing deeply as I watched the trees sway in the coastal air. I watched the rolling waves spill onto the sand under my feet at the ocean's edge. I silently thanked the universe for releasing me from a prison of my own choosing and asked for blessings upon the glorious future that awaited me.

I once worked with a wise spiritual coach who told me that spirit will tap us on the shoulder to get our attention, but if we refuse to listen, that tap may become a spiritual two-by-four. I had been singularly focused on my law firm's success and thought I was following my life's path, but I ignored the little taps from my soul as it tried to show me an alternative path—one led by feeling the joy and love of my family, the reward of helping others in my spiritual business, and the peace of a quiet life along a beautiful coastline. When I didn't listen to those gentle taps, the spiritual two-by-four upended my life to send me in a new direction.

Eight years ago, I would have insisted that manifesting my professional success was the culmination of my dreams. And yet, as I chained myself to what I thought was my life's purpose, my soul knew better and manifested a magical future that I simply couldn't see on my own. Our souls are powerful, and they will manifest our highest good whether our human wants to cooperate or not. If we meet our souls halfway by acknowledging those gentle taps, we can harness the magnificent power of our soul's manifestation ability. Pay attention to the whispers of your soul, and your soul will reward you with more beauty, love, joy and fulfillment than you could even imagine.

Bio

Karen Gabler is an award-winning attorney, intuitive mentor, psychic medium, animal communicator and Reiki master. She is also a best-selling author, teacher and inspirational speaker. Karen is passionate about encouraging others to find their highest purpose and live their best lives. She mentors her clients through a variety of personal and business issues, marrying her practical legal and business experience with her innate intuitive ability to receive information and guidance from higher sources. She also facilitates connections with clients' loved ones in spirit. Karen conducts workshops and presentations on a variety of business, spiritual and personal development topics. She earned her Bachelor of Arts in Psychology from the University of Hawaii and her Juris Doctorate from the William S. Richardson School of Law at the University of Hawaii. Karen has pursued wide-ranging education in interpersonal development and the spiritual sciences, working with tutors from the prestigious Arthur Findlay College for the Psychic Sciences in England as well as with numerous intuitives and mediums throughout the United States. She is a WCIT in the Martha Beck Wayfinder life coaching program. Karen enjoys reading, hiking, horseback riding and spending time with her husband and two children. You can find Karen at www.karengabler.com.

Chapter 11

Skipping a Step
By Sarah Gabler

Many people have a general understanding of manifestation. Vision boards, believing in yourself, setting intentions, asking spirit for help; there are many ways to manifest your desires. As long as you check all these boxes, you're good to go! But what happens when you start relying too much upon manifestation, forget the steps that really matter, and begin to spiral into unhealthy habits?

I started going to personal development retreats and studying spiritual practices when I was just 10 years old. At those events, I learned about manifestation, and it became one of my most-used tools. Throughout my day-to-day life, manifesting helped me to achieve so many things. I manifested finding my beautiful dog Beau, speaking at my 5th grade promotion ceremony, playing the lead in my middle school musical, admission to my chosen college, and more. In late 2019, however, manifestation became less of a powerful tool and more of a lingering trigger. Ironically, my manifestation practice manifested itself into an endless anxiety loop in my head and made me a nervous wreck.

The COVID-19 pandemic was a difficult time for everyone around the world. Every day brought stories recounting tragedies arising from the virus. This caused me immense stress, as I'm sure it did for others. As an empath who loves her family more than anything, I became incredibly scared of the virus. To avoid losing those I loved, I decided to use manifestation to bring safety to my family. Every night, I imagined my family in full health while living our best lives. This worked well for a bit, but I soon began to feel that if I didn't do my manifestation work every night, something bad would happen to my loved ones.

My fear became so great that instead of practicing my routine only at night, I manifested every time I heard another news story about COVID. This became exhausting. Because COVID filled the news at the time, I was reciting manifestations almost every ten minutes, which drained my energy. I felt solely responsible for maintaining the health of my entire family. I told myself that this was just pandemic stress and that once the world returned to normal, I would be able to relax.

As the pandemic crisis lessened and normal news stories reappeared, I noticed I was manifesting to avoid every possible danger. If I saw a story about drowning, I would manifest for safety around water. If I heard of someone passing of old age, I would manifest long lives for my family. If I heard of transportation crashes, I would manifest for safe travel. Manifesting became my full-time job, and ultimately made me unable to cope with hearing anything negative.

This continued when the pandemic isolation ended, and I returned to school. When my friends talked about a student getting COVID, I would step out of the conversation and start manifesting. After the pandemic ended, when my friends joked about anything remotely related to injury or death, I had to step away to manifest something positive. I felt so defeated that I couldn't handle being part of seemingly normal conversations.

What frustrated me the most was that I felt I didn't have a choice. I *had* to manifest. If I didn't, then I was letting those negative words enter the universe and something bad would happen. Why was one of my strongest tools turning into my worst enemy? I accepted that manifesting was no longer a space to make me feel protected and guided. It was now an exhausting cloud hovering above my head, constantly weighing me down with anxiety. I had to be doing something wrong!

I researched more about manifesting and soon realized that I wasn't doing anything wrong in wanting to manifest for the highest good of myself and my family, but I was manifesting from my head instead of my soul. I had turned manifestation into superstition, running myself through preordained steps to ward off evil and pain. By allowing myself to believe that I was the sole director of all of life's decisions and actions, I had forgotten that true manifestation taps into the power of our soul, who knows exactly who we are and what we're meant to do. I had forgotten that one of the most important parts of manifesting is trusting that everything meant for me is already on its way to me.

I realized that manifesting doesn't mean physically or mentally shifting your life and demanding that everything must go exactly the way you want it to go. Instead, it means connecting with your soul's plan and aligning yourself with the energy you want to bring into your life. It's asking your spirit guides to travel with you, helping to move obstacles from your path and shepherding you through your challenges. It's tapping into your soul energy and inviting the universe to align with your intentions, asking for guidance to keep you on track.

I would be lying if I said I no longer struggle with differentiating between my head and my soul. Trusting your soul's guidance is easier said than done. It can sometimes feel like the only way to remain in control is to clench your fists and squeeze your eyes shut to manifest for or against every possible thing that could happen in life. When you let go of your human need to control your environment and tap into your inner knowing, recognizing that you are held, supported and loved at all times, you will be guided to what will ultimately be your highest and best good.

If you find yourself in situations where you feel out of control and want to hyper-manifest every element of life, try a few simple practices that have helped me to feel less anxious about life's challenges:

Take some deep breaths and center yourself while sitting quietly. It can be overwhelming when life feels scary or out of control. It feels like you are in a tornado of your own mind. Stepping back and collecting yourself is the first step to finding clarity. The easiest way to hear your soul's voice is to quiet your mind's chatter.

Tap into your soul and feel into what you want in the moment. Don't put too much pressure on being right. Simply imagine what will make you feel the most fulfilled and set your intention accordingly. Let your soul drive your desires rather than your mind.

Trust that you are always guided and supported by your spirit helpers. Once you've set your intention, invite your spirit guides to lead you to your highest and best good based on what you have envisioned. Ask your guides to work out any obstacles along your path.

Accept that you've done what you can and trust that it is enough. At the end of the day, life has its ups and downs, and it is often unpredictable. I've learned the hard way that manifesting must be quality over quantity, and streamlining your manifestation routine will be beneficial to your overall mental health. If you connect with your soul and trust in your spirit guides, everything will fall into place.

Manifesting is a mighty tool if used correctly, but when it is overused or misinterpreted, it can lead to feeling stuck in a never-ending anxiety loop. Remember that you are never alone in this life. Your soul knows the path that has been laid out for you, and you have so many spirit helpers who will guide you every step of the way, loving and supporting you no matter what. Trust in yourself and in the guidance available to you, and know that when you are aligned with your soul, everything in your highest and best good will come to you with ease.

Bio

Sarah Gabler is 17 years old and is a senior in high school. She adores spending time with her family and traveling to new places. Sarah loves playing ukulele, guitar, and keyboard, and riding or spending time with her horse. Sarah is a lifelong artist and loves using creative outlets to express herself. She is an internationally best-selling author and has contributed her work to multiple published collections of short stories with As You Wish Publishing.

She works as a stage manager for her school productions and loves bringing shows to life to entertain others. Sarah plans to major in psychology and wants to study abroad during her college years. She began exploring spiritual teachings, self-development, and soul empowerment concepts when she was 10 years old and believes it has made her a better person today. It has motivated her to pursue her best life as well as to help others on their fulfillment journey. Sarah wants to empower people by helping them to recognize their true potential. She believes that even the smallest acts of kindness can make someone's day, and she always tries her best to help others feel heard, seen, and loved.

Chapter 12

What a Ride! The Journey Continues

By Maria Gigliotti

Hello all, my name is Maria, and this is my journey. I am a mother to an amazing son who has inspired me, taught me and guided me, and I could not be more grateful he chose me. I have family that has learned that I create my own path and love me nonetheless.

I, like many others, often wondered what if I knew then what I know now. This journey has taught me that I simply could not have known then. I have needed exactly every step of my awakening for the evolution of my mind and soul. My life choices and experiences were often questioned by others as to why she would do that or what happened to her.

Quite frankly, I often wondered about that myself. Gratefully, clarity has come through my opportunities to dig and expand from the deeper, more meaningful and spiritual place. Here is what I can now see as the driftwood along the way to today.

My moment of awakening began when I was able to accept pain as part of the process. I learned of the value of pain as I was exploring what I wanted and needed. Childhood for me had a lot of sadness and loneliness, and I wanted to embrace that and understand its purpose. I had plenty of moments that felt irrational and unrecoverable and where the darkness prevailed. However, there were often well-timed interactions that created a sense of hope and connection for me. The hope offered me connections I had felt too afraid to accept before. In retrospect, I see the connections leading to manifestation, but being vulnerable and trusting were significant obstacles for me. There have been numerous retreats where I found myself in tears over the connections I experienced and the a-ha moments I received.

One of the most amazing parts of this process has been the manifesting that has occurred in ways I barely paid attention to. There have been so many thoughts and situations which created a deep feeling in my soul at the times they occurred. Then, like many others, I moved on to whatever was next in my world. What I know today is that those experiences created intentions. Those intentions have now manifested, and I had forgotten I asked. For example, my spoken intention to be my own boss and create quality time with my son were statements made somewhat in passing, yet both have manifested. Then, in a moment, my breath is taken as I truly feel the power of the universe.

The opportunity to overcome limiting beliefs has provided me with a tremendous amount of respect and gratitude for the universe. When people have said to me that the universe keeps giving you the same lesson until you learn it, I did not want to see that. I had to keep reflecting and digging each time to find what limiting belief was in my way. Ultimately, for me, the limitation was based on a lack of self-worth.

A recent example of this is clear. I have a habit of saying yes to professional opportunities that excite me without thinking about it. Fortunately, these knee-jerk responses have been driftwood to moments of self-worth and trust. I agreed to speak to a large crowd that scared me to death. Gratefully, my trust in the process has consistently been enough to outweigh the fear. I wanted to cancel for many days, but trusting the process was the key. Ultimately, I faced that fear head-on. I came out the other side knowing I was given that opportunity because I am worthy.

Worthiness has been a foreign belief to me, but this opportunity solidified that my worth is what manifested this opportunity and its outcome. I knew it in my heart and soul. That was all the truth I needed. The universe sees my worth, and I never need to play small. I had no clue of the way the universe viewed me or even how others may have had positive perceptions of me. As I connected with more like-minded souls, I saw and felt the shift. I continue to face this limiting belief from time to time and have no doubt I will continue to overcome the false belief. I have deeply needed similar souls to show me my light and teach me how to harness it. I have been practicing a tapping exercise I learned from Gabby Bernstein, and the freedom is priceless.

I have explored and implemented many practices and rituals on my road to awakening. There are some that stuck and some that did not. I do my best to explore and not make judgments about what feels right for me at any given time. I have learned that if my intention is clear and powerful, the rest takes care of itself. I choose cards and crystals to start my day and clear my mind of distractions. I appreciate the direction such things can give to my presence and frame of mind. I learned to practice vulnerability and be present, neither of which had been part of my wheelhouse prior.

Adversity has been a key piece to molding my spiritual practice and journey. As a drug-addicted, 25-year-old college-educated, middle-class woman, I faced adversity through others' perceptions and judgments. I was criticized by a judge who believed I should have known better than to use drugs because I had a college degree. Unfortunately, education matters none, and that message has reverberated from others. I spent time in rehab, jail and supportive living to begin to build myself up again. The path has included trauma recovery and a lot of self-forgiveness. These areas are not fully resolved, but I stay focused on that success when I am faced with another challenge or adversity. I do, however, believe that adversity has made me stronger and better able to believe in myself. Loneliness presented itself again through this adversity, so my choice was to learn to at least like myself, with the goal of self-love.

My job has provided me endless opportunities to share my wisdom. I have worked in mental health settings for well over 20 years and feel blessed to have done so. I do not need to share my entire story with people for us to be able to relate to one another. I am open and vulnerable as needed and feel this to be one of my greatest gifts in which I can share my wisdom. I am an energy woman through and through, and I have no doubt that is evident in my work with others. I can confidently and genuinely share that they can recover and embrace the most beautiful parts of themselves.

I continue to grow spiritually through my never-ending desire to connect. I attend retreats when I can to get the best feelings to take back to my corner of the world. My day-to-day practices of working with crystals, pulling a card, tapping, or meditating are staples in my spirit.

After many years as a therapist, I have now started a new adventure. I have begun to delve into the world of leadership, self-leadership in particular. I own Crossroads Consulting Services and desire to help make personal and spiritual work interlace with our work environments. Crossroads Consulting Services is a direct manifestation of conversations, hopes and dreams along my road. I strive to help people explore their own souls, see their light and bring it everywhere they go. As a coach, I am truly honored to accept the invitation to walk with people from exactly where they are to where they deserve to go next.

I fully intend to keep reflecting, leaning in, and embracing this work. I look forward to continuing to be who I am on a soul level and bringing me to all my relationships. I hope to inspire others to trust and see what they deserve so they can shine their light.

Bio

Maria Gigliotti is an entrepreneur and owner of Crossroads Consulting Services. She can be reached at crossroadsconsultingservices.com and would love to chat. She thanks every soul on her road so far.

Chapter 13

Manifesting the Perfect Job: Magical Endings

By Lindsay Godfree

I was depressed. It felt like I had always been depressed and that it was never going to get better. I was dragging my right leg because my knee was not working. I asked myself, "How can I go on with my life?" It was a dark time, and worse because my life was good overall.

I was on a cruise ship taking the trip of a lifetime, cruising through the Panama Canal. I could hardly walk, and I couldn't be happy. I wasn't enjoying this beautiful environment or my life. I learned that Louise Hay wrote that knee problems are a result of fear of the future. I was stuck and experiencing what is called a "dark night of the soul."

At my wit's end, I brought a book with me that my sister gave me on infinite possibilities. I was then introduced to the idea of surrendering to infinite love and following inspiration and intuition. I made a commitment that I was not going to do anything without divine guidance.

I wanted to manifest the perfect job for me. I was determined to apply the law of attraction and work the magic of the universe to work things out. When I got home, I applied for many jobs. I imagined what it would feel like to have work that gave me a sense of purpose, joy, and fulfillment, and I trusted that what was best would appear. This process involves incorporating positive thoughts with appropriate feelings and imagining the life that you want.

A job I wanted appeared in an ad for a tour driver at Pink Jeeps, a local touring agency that would take people to beautiful places on adventure rides. I thought this would be my dream job, and I was ecstatic. I believed I was the perfect candidate since I had just completed two summers driving tour buses in Alaska. The only downfall was that I would be gone for long hours and could not help my mother. I had a phone interview that went very well. Excitedly, I waited for the magic to happen. Sadly, I was not their final choice and did not get a job offer.

"What next?" I asked the universe disappointedly. If this was not the best solution to moving forward in my life, what was it?

I was determined and willing to believe and be led by spirit. I took the actions explained in the book, taking baby steps toward getting a job. I did things like dress for success and imagined myself being happy and productive, filling out more job applications. Just as my unemployment ran out, I finally got an offer. It was not what I thought I wanted, but it was what had appeared, and I needed the work, so I went across town to the interview.

The valet company was so excited to have me, and it was great to feel needed and appreciated. Two major requirements of the imagined perfect job would be met here. I had doubts; this job was only part-time and was not the career step I thought I deserved. Despite my confusion, I settled in to see how the magic appeared. How would situations line up to help me reach my goals and find happiness?

The job entailed driving a shuttle for a large hospital. I was to shuttle the employees to and from their vehicles parked in various parking lots to get to their shifts at work. It turned out that I enjoyed the driving and the simple job of going around and around on my route in downtown Phoenix. I was stress-free at work even though I did not make much money. Although I liked my work, there was a growing uneasiness about the lack of a sense of purpose.

I asked spirit what I could do to make a difference where I was. The intuitive answer that came to me was that I could build a spiral, a forcefield, around and around the hospital where I could call angels to bless those who were sick, who were passing from life, and those who were grieving. This is when I felt a deep sense of purpose and connection to the divine that I was looking for. This feeling would help me break the spell of my depression.

I began trying to connect with the angels I learned about in my childhood. I believed that I did not know how to talk to them or call them in. I began researching prayers to address angels and discovered that one does not "pray" to angels but "invokes" them. Invoking is asking with the authority we ultimately possess as energetic beings. I learned that humanity is gifted with guardian angels as "sons and daughters" of God, or the Divine Source as the Creator. Angels are forcefields of energy assigned to watch over us and help us whenever we ask them to.

I decided that this was to be a research project to begin working with the angels and that I would want to document it. I deduced that I should compile what I was learning into a book. Maybe this would be how the universe would take me to my desired work and purpose in life. Maybe I would finally be happy.

I was just getting comfortable in the job and getting in the groove of what I was doing, and my supervisor asked me to transfer to the shuttle at the Mayo Clinic and Hospital on the other side of town. "There goes my spiral of energy," I thought. What was this new job going to be? It turned out that I would be driving the patients back and forth on a 30-minute one-way trip from the clinic to the hospital. It was more responsibility but not more money. I could not see how I would be closer to solving the problem I thought was my life.

I realized that I should be grateful. I was intuitively drawn to a book on gratitude called *The Simple Abundance Journal of Gratitude*. I purchased it with the few dollars that I had in my bank account. I eagerly awaited the book that would give me the answers to gratitude and increase my income, too.

I was so excited when it arrived! I opened a book of blank pages with just a few quotes scattered through it. Blank lined pages? What mean joke was the universe playing on me? Now I was angry. I was doing what I was directed to, and God gave me an empty book? I did not have the money to buy another book, so there was nothing to do but begin filling it out. Sullenly, I read the rules: write five things each day, and do not duplicate anything you already said. This was mission impossible!

I began by getting to work a little bit early each morning to start this new job and make my gratitude list. I was cranky about it. On the first day, I couldn't think of five things to be grateful for. But I continued and was amazed that it began to get easier each day. I learned to count the small things: the flowers that bloomed, the birds that sang, the sunshine, and the rain. Soon, it was difficult to limit my list to only five things to be grateful for.

Next, strange things started to happen; a lady in a wheelchair insisted she needed to shake my hand. Another lady with an angelic light in her eyes kissed me as she disembarked my van. I began to smile and even found a skip in my step.

One day, I came home from work and began to walk down the street to visit my mother in the next block. Suddenly, I realized that I was happy, truly happy, even if nothing ever changed. It was then that my life was changed forever. It hit me like a bolt of lightning. I was transformed into a new person. The magic of awakening occurred at that moment as I shifted into my multidimensional self.

It turned out that I did find the perfect job for me. Was this the end of the story? Truthfully, the magic of life never ends, and the story continues.

Bio

Lindsay S. Godfree is a best-selling author and creator of the Consciousness Guide. She is also a Channel of Angels and more.

The full story of her awakening experience is documented in "Awakening Consciousness – Finding a Larger Version of Self." The second edition, available in the Spring of 2024, includes workbook pages.

Also available in 2024 is a marvelous book of Lindsay's Channeled Angel Messages that are truly miraculous. Lindsay offers angel readings and courses on intuition, healing, and changing your consciousness at lindsaygodfree.com.

She lives in Arizona and is currently working on helping to establish the Healing Energy Ranch in Prescott. Email lindsay@lindsaygodfree.com

Free meditations from the angels at
https://lindsaygodfree.com/free-gifts/

Chapter 14

The Sacred Sparrow Soars

By GG Rush

Once upon a time, there was a very small bird's nest on a very high branch in a very tall tree in my own backyard. Over many years, I looked at that nest and wondered if it would ever hold any eggs or any life at all. Over those years, I often thought of that nest as I toiled at a job that I didn't love. A job that brought me payment and security but no fulfillment in my life. I knew in my heart and soul that I was destined for more. I felt a strong sense that I needed to be of service in some way. I needed to be able to feel a sense of accomplishment and happiness at the end of the workday. I also didn't want what I was doing to feel like work. Impossible, right? I just continued to go through the motions, one foot in front of the other, day after day.

I traveled to faraway lands, saw beautiful places, ate exotic food, and met so many wonderful people. I attended seminars and workshops where, even though I admired them all, I also felt jealous and envious that they were doing what I wanted to do with my life—being of service, teaching, inspiring and bringing peace to me. I read books written by all of them. I studied their methods and techniques, their modalities and manners. I once stood on one of the stages before the start of an event and felt a powerful urge to start speaking. I didn't. That would look weird, even among fellow weirdos, but I knew that I, too, could do this work and that I just needed to find my place. This went on for more than a decade. I spent thousands of dollars just to be in that same space with those golden gurus. I met so many like-minded souls, and I kept many of them as close friends. I would return home and go back to my job and my life feeling inspired. I was inspired until it wore off, and I was feeling defeated and beaten, my ideas dismissed and scoffed at by my "real world" people. I kept my dream inside me, and I prayed and meditated and manifested that someday it would be real. That I would be doing what I was meant to do with my life.

I am not saying I wasn't feeling totally unfulfilled. I continued to study, taking classes and seminars that gave me certifications. Unbeknownst to me, I was actually building my resume for my future. I studied for years under my Reiki Master, working my way through her Reiki classes and eventually earning my Reiki Master and Teacher certification. I studied hypnotherapy with the Schaefer Institute of Hypnosis, earning that certification as well as my Life Coaching certification. I took a clutter and space-clearing seminar with Denise Linn and went to that one, too. During this era of my life, I became a published author in several compilation books and eventually wrote a book on my solo travels. I then finally wrote down a story I had written for my daughters when they were little, and it became a published children's book. So yes, I was making inroads into my dream after all.

All these things were going on in my life, but still, I had to put on a brave face every weekday and go to that unfulfilling job. I'd been there nearly fifteen years, and I had great benefits and a very nice salary that allowed me to continue to travel and attend classes. But my unhappiness during those hours made me feel depressed and sad. I just knew I needed to find a way out. To live my dream life and earn enough money to survive.

Serendipity decided to call on me early in the year 2022. A cruise I had booked to Egypt was canceled. My wanderlust was strong, and I kept thinking of alternatives since I had tons of vacation days off. A teacher and friend that I admired brought up Hawaii, where she lives and runs life retreats. I didn't hesitate to book a flight and book the hotel in Kona Kailua on the Big Island of Hawaii. I spent days lounging by the pool, relaxing on the balcony, looking at the breathtaking view, and completing my children's book. I ate fabulous fresh seafood, tuna poke and fruit. I sipped tropical drinks. I took a full-day tour around the island, taking in the coffee plantations, the volcanoes and the waterfalls. I was calm and at peace, and I felt that something big was coming.

I met with my friend, Dr. Lisa Thompson, for a full afternoon in my hotel room. We chatted about my hopes and dreams. She read my soul cards and did a past life regression with me. We talked about my fears of leaving my job and starting my own business. As we talked on the balcony, there were so many little birds landing on the railing, watching us and looking for crumbs from my granola bar. I asked Lisa what kind of birds they were. Sparrows, Hawaiian sparrows.

When I left the island and began my long trip home to North Carolina, I contemplated what my future would be. To my own surprise, I felt it was so easy, and I made a very firm and confident decision about what I was going to do. When I returned to the office on Monday morning, the first thing I did was type out my two-week resignation. When I handed my three bosses those sheets of paper, they were shocked. They never ever thought I would up and quit. I was sixty-four, and I had talked before about retiring and collecting my social security, but I would hopefully wait until after I turned sixty-six or seventy. I knew in my heart that I would never be able to do that much longer. My health and happiness were suffering from the stress of that job.

And so it was. I gave two weeks' notice. I was a little scared, but I knew I had done the right thing for myself. That week, I had my monthly Reiki session with my Reiki Master, Marina. I told her that I had quit my job, applied for social security and was not sure what would happen next. She didn't miss a beat. She invited me to come onboard as her apprentice and use the open room she had so I could begin practicing immediately! She would also train me as a Reiki teacher! Wow! One door closes, and the universe opens the next one. The one of my dreams!

I needed a name for my practice. It popped into my head without any thought. Sacred Sparrow. I had a vision of that day on the balcony with Lisa and those little sparrows. It was perfect. I messaged my friend Tammy Cantrell, a website and business wizard. She designed my logo and created my website, and the rest is now up to me. She helped me with doing a business launch and keeps encouraging me to succeed. It hasn't been easy, but I have had the world's best help every step of the way.

I am so happy now. My life has completely changed. I am in charge of my time and my success. I graduated from Reiki teacher training and will start to train the next generation of Reiki practitioners. I do work I love, but I don't feel like it is work at all. I feel good helping my clients, whether it is with a Reiki session, a life coaching session or taking control of their space. I have incorporated past life regression with the use of my hypnotherapy training. I am excited to see this little business continue to grow. I haven't been on stage *yet*, but it is coming, I am certain. I have done some podcast interviews, and I will look at doing my own podcast.

One of my favorite sayings is, "It's never too late to be what you might have become." It is real. Way up high in that tree in my own backyard, a little egg hatched. And a Sacred Sparrow soared higher and higher into the sky. Limitless and free. Spread your own wings and fly!

Bio

GG Rush is an author, Certified Life Coach, Clinical Hypnotherapist and Clutter Clearing Coach. She is a certified Reiki Master and has studied Aromatherapy,

Chakra Balancing, Toxic Emotions and the ancient art of Pulse Reading. She has traveled the world solo and will continue her journey to see the world and find herself. GG, aka Gail Rush Gould, resides in Cary, North Carolina, with her cat Bella. Her coaching website is SacredSparrowSpiritual.com.

Chapter 15

The Spiritual Mack Truck

By Katherin Elli Grace

I was late joining the spiritual awakening party. In fact, I could have missed it all together. Nearing 60 years old, I was stubborn and resistant, dragging my feet, white-knuckling it, trying to control every aspect of my life. I was comfortable in my comfort zone.

I was deeply rooted in disbelief and self-reliant behavior and didn't stir from my spiritual coma until I was in my 30s when I met Loretta. She was a local psychic who taught me about Hawaiian metaphysics. She had me at Aloha. I was fascinated. Something stirred inside. I wasn't ready to let go of my skepticism, but I was coming around.

Many of the next years were spent in a haze as I shifted into my spiritual seeker phase. Childhood fears and limiting beliefs were taunting me. I was depressed and anxious. Feeling broken and not good enough, I decided to test Loretta's spiritual way of living. I began my search, running from healer to healer, trying every modality I could find. I was looking desperately for somebody or something to fix me. I just wanted to be at peace.

I found lots of Band-Aids, but none stuck. My life always reverted back to the pain and heartache I was trying to heal. I wasn't doing the inside work my spirit team had been guiding me to do. I was looking outside of myself for the love that would heal me. I couldn't heal myself because I didn't love or accept myself. I would stay stuck on my path for many more years to come. Unaware that healing occurs when you awaken your inner magic.

In my late 50s, the perfect storm was brewing. My depression and anxiety ramped up, and I felt alone and in despair. I was entrenched in victimhood and a frequent guest at self-pity parties. All aspects of my life were unraveling. I was struggling to keep going. My resilience was waning.

That's when my spirit team took control, seeing that I was gripping the wheel and spinning out of control. My life was spiraling down. Every aspect of my life seemed to be in turmoil. That's when my spirit team brought in the spiritual Mack truck, and it hit me and proceeded to run me over. I was done. I couldn't get up, and that's when I surrendered.

After all the years of sprinting through life, I was exhausted, and something inside kicked in, and I knew my time was up.

I felt something deep within shift. It came with a knowing that it was time to wake up. I had much more to do. This wasn't a message I could ignore. My spirit team had made it glaringly clear to me that my rigid ways of living weren't working. I needed to make changes now.

So, I found that invitation to the spiritual awakening party I had buried and ignored. I RSVP'd with a resounding yes! I began my next journey with a travel magazine that I had subscribed to 30 years prior. But as I began making new choices, my negative limiting belief playlist started blaring—you can't afford to travel, you're single, you're too old—trying to hold me back.

This time was different; my strength was bubbling up, and something took over. I booked the relocation tour offered on the first page. I looked at and visited Panama the next month. I spent the next year happily engrossed in preparing for the next chapter of my life. I was taking charge, not making fear-based decisions or listening to that old playlist. I refused to have any regrets when my time was up.

The date neared to submit my notice of resignation. Excitement abounded, and I was encouraged and motivated to move forward with this new adventure, an opportunity to immerse myself in a new culture to grow. I was done with my Ground Hog Day existence, sitting on the couch watching TV, crying and feeling sorry for myself.

So in July of 2018, I handed in my resignation, sold or donated my stuff, my material possessions and on August 25th, 2018, I touched down in Panama with 3 suitcases and a duffle bag to start the next chapter of my life at age 62. I've learned living life the spiritual way in alignment with your heart and soul is a better way to live on my journey to awaken my magic.

Bio

Katherin Elli Grace is a retired RN of 40+ years who left her comfort zone in New York and set off on a journey to expand her horizons in tranquilo Panama. Immersing herself in the culture has provided her with many new adventures and opportunities for growth and making new friends from across the world. She has been supportive of her new country through her volunteerism with various organizations. In addition to travel, her interests include creative design projects, decorating and music, and socializing. She loves all things woo-woo, especially unique healing modalities. Her heart's passion is being a support and inspiration for others, like herself, who experienced childhood abuse and trauma and are now ready to leave their comfort zones behind and awaken their magic. After the information she received in a Soul Contract Reading profoundly changed her life, she became a certified practitioner in it and its counterpart, Divine Healing.

She can be reached by email at:
Katherin@KatherinElliGrace.com.

Chapter 16

Ambassadors of Love

By Lisa Guess

I don't proclaim to know the secrets of the universe, but I have extensive knowledge of compassion and, most importantly, empathy. Compassion is defined as the sympathetic pity and concern for the sufferings and misfortunes of others. Empathy is defined as the ability to understand and share the feelings of another.

How can one understand and share the feelings of another? In psychology, an empath is a person who has a higher-than-usual level of empathy, referred to as hyperempathy. It's not a condition or a superpower that one can obtain through simply trying. Although I do understand it can be more difficult for some than others.

I can remember as a child, I was very sensitive, and I could feel shifts in the emotions of others. If a person was sad, happy or mad, I could sense it. It was all in the eyes. I can still walk into a room and completely disregard the latest fashion and feel only the energy of the room. Whether or not the person is kind is always my first and last impression. Maybe that's why I became a nurse.

I knew I wanted to make a change in this world. I have always felt kindness was the way. I wasn't wrong. Twenty years later, kindness wins every single time. I decided I would be a voice for those hurting or in need of a voice. I talked to my dear friend Beth about my idea of reaching others through a book, and this is the result of that conversation. The term Ambassador of Love came out of my mouth, and as soon as I said it, my heart listened.

What do we need in this world? Ambassadors of Love. Where does it begin? At home with our children. The art of empathy can be learned and taught at any age.

As a nurse for twenty years, I've seen a lot of tragedy and loss. I've been privileged to be in a room when a soul takes their first breath and as a soul takes their last. I've held the hands of the dying and comforted them. I hugged the families as they said goodbye to their loved ones. I have also found that all deaths aren't the same. The child dying of cancer versus the 98-year-old patient whose family is there as a testament to her life is not the same. I learned really quickly that life isn't fair, and neither is death. It's a trigger for me to even bring this up as I see their faces and know in my heart I did all I could do. But in the end, we all face death. We all face challenges, and we all hurt.

When I think of how unfair life is, I immediately think of children with disabilities that limit their ability to talk, walk, eat or even scratch their noses without assistance. All the things we take for granted on a daily basis are a struggle for them. As if diseases like this aren't enough, they're faced with the challenges of fitting into this society where anything that isn't perfect is considered imperfect and not good enough. One of the worst things I see parents do with their children is scold their child when they look at another child with a disability. It is normal for children to have questions and to look at people who are different. They want to know, so let them ask.

Parents of children born with disabilities are emotionally, mentally and physically drained. They need and deserve people in their lives who will support them. From the moment the diagnosis is given, it is a feeling of "What did I do wrong?" or "What could I have done differently?" It's a blame game, and they accept that blame 100% to the point of not attending to their own needs.

Nurses are brought into the home for assistance, but then the privacy of a normal household is gone. They share their home with strangers in shifts. Sometimes, they get lucky enough to find someone who fits into their home and treats their child with empathy like family. Imagine getting excited by the idea of sleeping through the night without worry. The equipment alone makes any trip a very complicated one. What did I forget? What if my child gets sick on the trip and their specialist isn't available?

If you see special needs parents, encourage them. Tell these parents they are doing a great job. Encourage your children to make friends with their child. There's so much to learn when others are different from you. Encourage your children to ask the questions. Encourage your children to make eye contact, and don't dismiss the other child by quickly looking away.

Can you, for one moment, imagine someone looking in your direction and being told by their parents to stop looking. At that moment, that person has been devalued by you, and no matter how much that child is loved at home, it only takes one moment to really change a good day for that child. I've witnessed the struggle, the pain and the tears.

Children with disabilities are, most of the time, very aware of their condition. They face the world head-on with bravery, which I am blown away by. They have moments of frustration, pain and sorrow. In the end, they truly only want to be accepted by others. I've heard many times from disabled children, "Why me? Why doesn't anyone want to be my friend? Why do people laugh at me or call me names? Why do people turn and walk the other way instead of talking to me? Why were they so mean? I just wanted to be their friend." All of these are valid questions and a source of more pain for these children. As if it's not enough to have a daily routine of medications, painful procedures and strangers come into their homes to care for them. Their lives are not easy. As a society, we must do better for these children and their families.

This is the part where I want to encourage you to be an Ambassador of Love. We must approach every situation with these two thoughts: what if that was me, and how would I feel? You're halfway there at that point. It's also easier said than done. Life comes at us hard and fast, and it's easy to get sidetracked. But if practiced at home, it can be an easier transition when the time comes. Teach your children to be Ambassadors of Love. A smile is the easiest and sweetest hello. Never tell them to look away; encourage them to engage with children with disabilities. Encourage your child to offer help with a door or to pick up something that might be dropped. Encourage your children to turn away from those who would find pleasure in the pain of others.

Kindness and love start at home. Instill within your children the strength to stand up for the child left out. As parents, we should reach out to the parents with a disabled child. The smallest things mean so much. Tell them what a great job they're doing. Get to know these people because they are strong. They're people you want in your life. They work hard and love even harder. They need breaks, and date night is so important for these couples. Life isn't fair. But the burden of life can be eased by the simple gesture of kindness. We need to start a movement for these children and their parents. We need Ambassadors of Love in every neighborhood, community, city and state. The world needs love now more than ever. I believe humanity still has a chance. Love, compassion and empathy are the answers.

Bio

Lisa Guess is a first-time author. She grew up in West Monroe, Louisiana. Lisa has been a nurse for 20 years. She has worked in many aspects of the nursing profession, including travel nursing in Minnesota, Montana, and Vermont. She held a title with Tulane Simulation Center in New Orleans, LA, as an AHA BLS Instructor for many years. Lisa enjoys advocating for animals and individuals for fair treatment. Lisa believes in being a voice for the voiceless and encourages all to become an Ambassador of Love. If you would like to reach out to Lisa, you may do so at lisakguess839@gmail.com

Chapter 17

I Didn't See the Sign at All

By Giulia George

My anxiety was through the roof. I felt like I was jumping out of my skin all day, every day for the past 3 weeks. I tried not to think the worst. I tried not to let my mind go there.

Every morning, I woke up thinking today will be the day it all changes. It all gets fixed. He comes to his senses. The anvil falls on his head. He wakes up. He says he's sorry. He comes home.

And every day, I go to bed fearing the worst, praying, praying, praying for the best and hoping for the gift of sleep to temporarily make these feelings go away, only to be reminded I am an insomniac. My son, my handsome, lanky, sharply witty, brilliant son, was, for lack of a better term, on the lam. That's what I told people, the ones who knew, to garner a laugh. But I wasn't laughing.

He couldn't take the restriction he was under and decided he wouldn't. As simple as that. Which meant there was a warrant out for his arrest. All because he had been driving with a suspended license, and they found marijuana and adder-all in his car.

So, now the boy whose parents walked the straightest of the straight and narrow had a son running from the law. We were beside ourselves. No amount of begging, pleading, cajoling, bribery, guilt, none of it made a difference. He was doing it his way, and "Mom, I'm a man, so don't worry." Sure.

On this particular day, I went about my methodical day. I woke up at 3:30am, hosted a popular morning radio show until 10am, went to the gym, and came home to my empty house. I took a shower, and I could feel the anxiety brewing. I got dressed and started to talk to myself, as I often did. But this time, I was talking to them—my deceased parents. My dad, specifically, who had been very close to my son and had died the year before. My guides, my guardian angels, Archangel Michael—anyone who would listen.

At first, I had a normal tone. But, as I kept talking, I began to get more and more excitable. I began to get louder, I started to get angrier, and then I began to shout. At the top of my lungs. "I need a sign!" "I need a sign that everything will be alright, that everything is going to work out, that he will be okay, that we will be okay, that all will be okay!" I kept shouting, "It has to be a real, bonafide sign. Do you hear me? In fact, it needs to be an actual sign. It can be on the back of a truck, on a wall, a billboard, anything, but I want a real sign that it will all work out!" I kept on shouting, all alone in my house. My voice echoed and bounced off the walls, "I simply can not take it anymore. I just need to know he'll be okay. Please, please, please give me a sign!"

I took a deep breath and thought to myself, if there was a peeping tom peering into my window, they would take off because surely the woman yelling at the top of her lungs to herself in her house was having a manic episode. I calmed myself down and grabbed my purse to run some errands around town. I scolded my guides or whoever was listening to my rant as I walked out the door.

"Okay, I'm getting in the car, and I'm going out. I better see a sign. Do you hear me? A real sign!" I got in the car and began driving. As I was driving, I kept saying out loud, "Okay, I'm looking. I'm on the hunt. I don't care what it is, but I have to see it." And I kept on looking, driving slowly, which is not the norm for me, searching for this sign. Unbeknownst to me, as I was 'looking' for the sign, I failed to notice the song on the radio. "I saw the sign, and it opened up my eyes. I saw the sign. Life is demanding without understanding. I saw the sign." I couldn't believe it.

I stared at the radio. And the tears just began rolling down my face. They had given me a sign. A real sign. And, of course, it was a song. I'm a radio personality. Of course, it would be a song. I often think songs that come on the radio are messages from them all the time. So, they did it. They heard me, and they sent me *The Sign* by Ace of Base.

Bio

Giulia George is a long-time South Florida radio personality who's been setting her alarm way before the chickens for over two decades. A mom of two who likes to exercise and indulge in all things new age.

Chapter 18

Manifesting The Love of My Life

By Sushma D.A. Hallock

School has always been my safety blanket. Ever since I can remember, I have always been in one class or another. After my undergrad studies and a lot of debt, I found myself working as a personal care companion to an elderly woman north of Toronto. On one of my breaks, I took a walk and found an alternative health store. That's when I saw an advertisement for a Reflexology course. I was intrigued. That was my first foray into the world of alternative healing. It was through this program that I met a massage therapist and started contemplating massage therapy as my next career goal. And so, before I knew it—I found a school close to home, took a tour and signed up! My parents were in complete shock! I had recently finished university, still paying off my student loans, and here I was, signing up for more school and, in their mind, more debt.

I cannot remember how I convinced them that this was a good thing for me. At that time, I did not connect that my sensitive nature was a part of my intuitive abilities. Unlike now, where I *feel or know* it's a good decision—back then, I didn't have a clue. I knew I was different from my other West Indian family members. As far back as I can remember, I was branded as *sensitive* and felt like I didn't fit in. All I had heard throughout my life was that I was *too emotional*—as if being emotional was a negative trait.

Massage school was a great experience. I loved learning about the human body and how massage therapy could help people from athletes, clients with fibromyalgia, people recovering from cancer, etc.—massage therapy changed my life. It was an incredible blend of both science and restorative healing.

In massage school, I discovered my excellent connection and networking skills, which I continue to use! I met a classmate who I was drawn to. She had a great sense of *knowingness* about her. It felt like she was an old soul. As students do, we started talking about what we wanted our futures to look like. For me, it was to find a steady job as a massage therapist and get married. One day, she told me about a method she used to help her achieve her dreams. At that time, I didn't know what manifesting was. I knew I wanted to get married and have kids—the typical path for South Asian females.

The method seemed straightforward: write down what I wanted in my future husband and then wait. I did customize it to fit my style. I used a large page from an art book, and I wrote the words *My Future Husband in* the center of the page and circled it. Then, I drew lines from those words outward with the characteristics of my future husband. He would be over 6'0", intelligent, loved to laugh and make me laugh, had a good job, etc.

Fast forward about five years. I'm still practicing as a massage therapist but am now teaching anatomy at a local college. I was doing well but still hadn't met the person of my dreams; however, I was making great progress on reducing my student debt and enjoying life with family and friends.

But I started getting the *feeling* that I needed to go to grad school. The universe was not subtle in letting me know where I needed to go. I started noticing signs about Massachusetts, specifically Boston. In the end, I followed my instincts and was accepted into Boston University School of Medicine. It was the only school I applied to through lots of hard work, and it was where I met the *love of my life*.

A part of my master's included acquiring MRI images, and this is how I met my future husband. He had to help run the MRI. We joke about how he was hiding and waiting for me in a dark basement since there were no windows where he worked.

Kevin was a rural, Midwestern guy, and I wasn't sure what to make of him. He was wicked tall—6'5"—you couldn't miss him. Plus, when I met him, I couldn't tell if he was cute or not. He had Einstein hair and wore jeans and a sweatshirt every day. Unlike me, he was a postdoc; I was starting my grad school journey, and he had finished his. He had a Ph.D. in Physical Chemistry and Biophysics. Before we go any further, let's review my wish list: over 6'0"—check 6'5"; he's smart—check Ph.D.; loved to laugh and make me laugh—double check; had a good job—he was a poorly paid postdoc, so I wasn't sure if he was *the one*.

In my master's program, I decided I wanted to become a medical doctor despite not liking germs. I started taking night classes for undergraduate chemistry on top of my graduate studies. And since Kevin was such a nice guy, he volunteered to be my chemistry tutor. Whenever I tell that story, people will chuckle and say, "Your chemistry tutor, eh?" They assume Kev had ulterior motives, but he was truly interested in helping me out. Kev is not an emotive kind of guy. During my time in grad school and chemistry classes, we spent a lot of time together. He would take his time when I didn't understand a chemistry question. After eight months of being friends, our relationship slowly evolved into something more. We started spending more time with each other, not because of my classes but because we wanted to hang out with each other. When we started dating, I told my dad that anytime we left the apartment, Kev would always put his hand out for me. My dad said, "Because he will always support you," and that is exactly how it has been ever since!

15 years later, we are still laughing with each other. We call each pet names. His is *Giant*, and I am Little Giant. Remember, he is 6'5", and I am almost 5'2". I'm sure you were wondering if we had little ones, alas, that was not in the stars for us, but that's a story for another time. What's most important is that we have each other. And he is truly *the love of my life*!

Bio

My name is Dr. Sushma D.A. Hallock. I was born in Guyana, South America (I identify as both West Indian and South Asian). My parents moved to Canada when I was a toddler—we lived in Calgary, Alberta and then Toronto, Ontario. I moved to Massachusetts for graduate school. Since moving here, I got married, completed a Master's in Anatomy & Neurobiology, an MBA and finally finished my doctoral work in Clinical Sexology with a focus on Sex Education in the fall of 2023.

In addition, I have taken many intuitive courses with Tony Stockwell, Ann Theato, Mavis Pittilla, and many more intuitive practitioners. I see myself as a voracious learner and an intuitive practitioner. I can connect with people on an intellectual level and on a soul-to-soul level.

Along my journey of self-discovery, I discovered that I am an *animal whisperer* and can communicate with animals, both present and those who have crossed over to the other side. I took a leap of faith, embraced my new skills, and eventually became *The Rainbow Bridge Medium.* I feel extremely blessed to know my purpose in life—to help every being have a voice! https://therainbowbridgemedium.com/

Chapter 19

Ditch, Dive, and Detach: How to truly live your greatest life

By Donna Kiel

What have you always wanted? Let me rephrase that: what have you always wanted that you have been too anxious to say out loud? What have you wanted that you just haven't made the time or strategy to get for you? What's been in your way? If you're like me, perhaps it was the long "to-do" list of life that includes work, family, laundry, and the biggie—fear.

For as long as I can remember, at least for five decades, I have believed that my life existed to make a difference in the lives of others. I found purpose and meaning in helping people, especially children. I had careers as a high school counselor, then a principal, a professor, and a life coach to serve and give to others. I was the daughter, mom, sister, and friend who all could rely on to remember everything, plan everything, and *always* be there to help. I began the journey of being the one to take charge and care for others when I was very young. At 6 years old, I was the one who took care of my infant brother with Down syndrome and taught him to walk and play. At the age of 13, before I had a driver's license or knew how to drive, I drove my dad, who was having a massive heart attack, to the hospital as my mom was having a panic attack.

Like many women, I became the one to always ensure that everyone's needs were met, from planning dinners to soothing broken hearts and helping everyone move into their new homes. Now, as a partner, mom, grandma, professor, and life coach, my schedule is a constant pattern of working 7 days a week and often 10 to 12 hours a day. I always feel like I'm behind, and I never have a completed "to-do" list. I am constantly checking email (I have 4 accounts to check), and if I just happen to be caught up with email, I can feel myself getting anxious as I have no one to help. I wake up each day determined to get everything done and help everyone. I end my day only when I am too exhausted to do any more.

As I describe my life, I realize how exhausting it was and yet how vigilant I was in continuing the pace and even adding more and more to my already full plate. That is, I continued until it all caught up to me. I had stopped my consistent practice of working out each day so I could work harder. I had also stopped taking days off or vacations. It started first with hip pain. Then, a routine MRI showed a spot that was a minor indication of potential stroke or dementia. I believed my plant-based diet, once-a-week yoga class, and walking the dog for 10 minutes each morning equaled a very healthy life. I was wrong.

When my doctor said exercise was the remedy, I thought, "Great, I can do that." I can get up earlier. Then she said, "More importantly, you need to eliminate stress, stop working so hard, and get more sleep." I could feel my chest tighten as she told me I needed to rest, to relax, and the dreaded words, "Take care of yourself." I also foolishly believed I was different. I didn't need as much rest as others because I was doing important work and taking care of everyone.

I believed, mistakenly, that I was a Wonder Woman and could outlive any type of limitation. It was in the middle of a therapy session, when my therapist said to me, "What exactly are you waiting for to do what you have wanted to do?" I had one of those moments that made time stop. I wasn't doing what I wanted to do because I was too busy doing it for everyone else so that I would be loved and valued.

I realized at that moment, that time was running out. I was not living my truest life. I was living a life for everyone but me. I realized that my saying yes to every project, every request, and every situation was doing nothing but depleting me and making me lose myself. In that moment, and with a great deal of vulnerability, I realized either I start to do for me, or I will never do what I want or live what is the true purpose of my life. That true purpose is to realize my dreams, my desires, and my joy.

I realized that God had given me this one life to live. This life was mine and no one else's. As the queen of responsibility and doing everything, I had neglected my responsibility to me. Now was my time, and I needed a dramatic, easy, and doable approach to living my greatest life.

I started by making a list of everything I wanted. I asked myself, what is my wildest dream, and what means the most to me? What is it that if I never get to do it, I will forever regret it? This is step one to living your greatest life. Ask what you want. List what you truly want. This is the important "ditch," which is step one. Ditch what gets in your way. For me, it was ditching the mistaken belief that I would not be loved if it took time for me. I needed to ditch the idea that the world would end if I didn't plan the meals for the holidays. I needed to ditch the excuses for not resting, not stopping work, and making myself always last. What do you need to ditch?

Then, using what I always teach others, I looked at my list and wallowed in the feelings I would have when those items came true. I named how I would feel when I wrote that book that told the truth about the Catholic school system. I lingered in that feeling of meaning and justice. I named how I would feel to spend days alone at a nature retreat. I lingered in that feeling of peace and calm. Step two is to dive into the positive feelings that you would have when you get what you truly want. Truly, dive in. Dive in and feel. Deeply feel your dreams coming true. Name the feelings. Name where you feel it in your body. Dive and wallow in the joy.

Most importantly, to live your greatest life is to de-tach. Yes, detach. Detach from thinking you can con-trol the outcome of anything. Detach from needing to please others, look a certain way, or have a certain title. Instead, attach to your dreams. The moment you let go is the moment you are truly within your truest self.

Right now, as you read this, begin your journey to ditch those beliefs that are not serving you. Dive into what you want to feel in this life. Detach from the mistaken notion you can control any outcome. Live your fullest, most joyful, and greatest life. Be you. Be true. Be love.

Bio

Dr. Donna Kiel is a teacher, activist, writer, and lover of spontaneous dancing and laughing. She is a life coach, speaker, executive coach, professor, and mentor. Donna has inspired thousands to gain self-awareness and achieve greater levels of personal and professional success. Her expertise in personal growth combined with educational theory and genuine compassion results in the unique ability to see in others what they may not see in themselves. She holds three degrees, including a BA in psychology, an MA in counseling, and a doctorate in leadership. Donna's specialties include life change, career success, personal fulfillment, anxiety reduction, confident public speaking, and aging with vitality. Donna works with individuals and groups. Donna offers free assessment and consultation for those seeking growth.

She can be reached at drdonnakiel@gmail.com or through her website at www.donnakiel.com.

Chapter 20

Heart Tribe

By Amy I. King

Driving home from cardio drumming last night, with tears rolling down my cheeks, I realized I had found my people. The loss of a friend from high school earlier that day had sent me reeling. When she arrived that night to drumming, Daina wrapped me in her arms and said, "We got you. No matter how you show up, we are here for you. We are your people." I had tried to pull away but stopped myself while in her embrace. Then Anita hugged me and told me she had worked in the funeral business and understood what I was going through. Christy bounded in with a giant hug, as well. One thing about this group is there is always a supply of support. This group of women is what I had been so desperate to find. Tears streamed down my face as I thought, "Wow, what a difference a few months can make."

I was at a dark and lonely point at the beginning of this year. Many relationships have disappeared as a result of COVID-19. However, I still had my best friend since high school. However, her true colors came out when she couldn't be bothered to check on me after surgery in December. The days following surgery were brutal, leaving me unable to keep anything down. Her text response of "Bummer" when I expressed my pain said it all.

Without blood family, my friends are my family. Alone, afraid, and unsure of what lay ahead, I turned to food as I had during the lonely months of the COVID lockdowns. I realize now that I had levied unfair expectations on people incapable of caring for themselves, so how could I expect them to care for me? I have learned that when someone shows you who they are, you must believe them the first time. She had shown me over and over again that she wasn't my person. I asked the universe/God/whatever you would like to believe is out there to bring me a group of women who are loving and supportive of one another. I kept asking night after night, "Please bring me a group of women who are loving and supportive of one another."

After spending my birthday in May alone, I decided never to do that again. I received flowers, candy, and phone calls from close friends wishing me happy birthday as I have a fantastic network of friends strewn about the country, but my local support system was minimal. I knew I had to make a change and that those women wouldn't just magically show up at my front door. It would require a level of vulnerability that I wasn't accustomed to, but I was willing to change to improve my life.

Scrolling through Facebook one day, I came across a girlfriends group. I joined and watched as events were posted, comments were made, and women were having fun together. Still, I didn't attend any of the events. Then, ageism crept into that group, and I searched for something else. I found another girlfriends group and was quickly sent a greeting by Darlene, a woman in her 60s with a warm smile and a commanding presence. Events were being posted, and I wanted to attend, but I needed to be more present. What if they don't accept me? What if I feel out of place? Middle age can be tricky for making new friends, and I wasn't ready for more rejection.

I saw a post about cardio drumming and inquired whether it would be something I could do from a seated position in my wheelchair. Darlene replied that it was possible, and she sat in a chair while drumming. I decided to be brave and attend that first class in early June this year. I nervously pulled into the wheelchair-accessible parking space in front of the building almost an hour before class was to start. I sat in my car until I saw Darlene park next to me. As she was getting out, I opened the door and began putting my wheelchair together. "Are you Amy?" She asked. "Yes," I replied.

She welcomed me with open arms as we entered The Studio Martial Arts building. I quickly filled out the waiver, and in I went. About 20 to 30 other women were drumming it out and having the best time. I met a few women that day and received more hugs than I had in a long while! I went home smiling. Each week, I came back for more. In early August, I joined some women for Drag Queen Bingo downtown. That night, I met Alicia, Cassandra, Cynthia, Anita, Kaitlyn, and Veronica. What a fun night! Then, in late August, Tim and Daina extended an invitation to their home for Labor Day and to celebrate Tim's Birthday. I met and got to know many beautiful women that day. We ate, talked, and played Left-Right-Center. I left their home feeling renewed.

Soon, Daina invited me to her bridal shower in September and Tim and Daina's wedding in October. I quickly became part of this loving and supportive network of women. There was no doubt in my mind that my lonely days were over.

Witnessing Tim and Daina's wedding and the subsequent joining of their families of six beautiful children, I cried tears of pure joy! I am now part of a unique tribe of women who support and show up for one another. I sometimes pinch myself because how can this possibly be real? Hugs are essential for our health, community is vital to our well-being, and mine now surrounds me!

My social life has gone from nearly non-existent to my calendar being so full that I almost don't have time to breathe. Recently, I drove up to Apple Hill with my new friends Alisha, Christy, and Betty. We ate apple donuts and apple fritters and drank a coffee flight. We had so much fun and some great laughs. Melissa and I attended the Janet Jackson concert, which was amazing! A few of us went to a Chippendales show. Oh, what a night!

This weekend, we have a baby shower for Alisha's daughter and a Friendsgiving celebration at Tim and Daina's. The change in my life is unbelievable, and the difference in my body is equally impressive. Every CD class ends with a group picture. I have saved every image. Last week, the photo was astounding. I quickly searched through my saved photos and found one of the pictures from the first sessions. I couldn't believe the difference! I posted them side by side.

My muscles are stronger, and my body is smaller due to cardio drumming and a challenge we have been in as a group to stay within our calorie needs to have a deficit, get 10,000 steps daily, and drink lots of water. We have been at it for five weeks, and I have felt my body shift. The change has happened over time, but the difference in my body, mind, and spirit is astounding. I no longer spend weekends with take-out in front of the television. I have devoted myself to cooking, eating healthy, exercising, sleeping, and drinking plenty of water. And I feel amazing! I whole-heartedly believe that what you think you deserve is what you attract. I started to believe that I deserved to be surrounded by women who supported me, and well, here they are. This group of supportive and lov-ing women is indeed a soft place to land. Sometimes, we must let go of what we thought we should have to have what we truly deserve. With the help of this fantastic group of women I now call friends, I am growing into the woman I'm destined to be.

Bio

Amy I. King is a Certified Life Coach/owner of Your Phenomenal Life, LLC. She is the best-selling au-thor of *Messy Wheels: Stories From Where I Sit* and contributing author of international bestsellers: *In-spirations: 101 Uplifting Stories for Daily Happiness, Manifestations: True Stories of Bringing the Imagined into Reality, The Grateful Soul: The Art and Practice of Gratitude, The Courageous Heart: Finding Strength in Difficult Times, Ordinary Oneness, Enduring Wisdom, 365 Days of Self Love, Whispers from the Heart, Wisdom Keepers*, and many more. When not writing, she enjoys improv classes, cardio drumming, music, movies, art, meditation, travel, and time spent with her chosen family.

Amy has overcome many challenges from which she draws wisdom to assist clients. Amy's greatest joy is using her experiences to help others move past their personal blocks and outdated beliefs to become empowered to live their dreams. Every challenge, she believes, is put before us to enable us to evolve and grow into the highest version of ourselves.

She builds relationships with clients based on trust and vulnerability. She welcomes the opportunity to help you transform your life!

Email her at Amy.kinglifecoaching@gmail.com.

Chapter 21

Surrounded by Gold

By Amy I. King

For over a year, I had felt like I would meet someone special who would change my life. My friend
Shawn confirmed my feelings when she slowly stat-
ed, during a healing session, "You are going to meet
a man in Maui who is surrounded by gold." After a series of bad relationships, I was at a low point, feeling
like I wasn't worthy of a quality relationship. I decided
to throw caution to the wind and planned a solo
trip. Ecstatic, I was ready for whatever adventure lay
ahead. Maui magic is undeniable.

The airport shuttle, complete with a wheelchair lift,
arrived at my door at the predicted time. I waved to
the driver, who I knew from previous trips. Noni got
out and readied the lift for me. I rolled, tightly holding
the handles on either side of the lift. I transferred

from my chair to the van's back seat as I asked how his family was doing.

We arrived at the airport and were greeted with the song "Walking on Sunshine" playing outside as if it were the day's soundtrack. Security was a breeze, although watching me go through the demoralizing pat-down proved too much for the sweet 60-something woman who, with her husband, was also traveling to Hawaii. The giveaway was their matching Hawaiian shirts. She began to cry as she watched from about 20 feet away.

Afterward, in line at Starbucks, she expressed her mortification. I assured her it was just part of travel for someone in my situation. She cried that it wasn't fair that they treated me as though my body wasn't mine. I agreed. But I love to travel, so I deal with it. I'm always first to board and last to disembark.

The flight lasted about 5 1/2 hours. I watched some movies, ate some decent food, and relaxed in anticipation of my big adventure. Using an airplane bathroom is challenging, so I do my best not to drink fluids before or during a flight. We landed in Honolulu, where I would transfer planes and head to Maui.

While waiting for the flight in Honolulu, I realized I could have booked the earlier connection. Good information for next time. Once we landed in Maui,

I retrieved my luggage, attached the large rolling suitcase to the back of my chair using a luggage strap, and fashioned it into a loop that would go through the side handle of the suitcase and around the back of my seat.

I laid the carry-on in my lap and secured it with my crossbody purse. I pulled my suitcase outside and went to the rental car shuttle area. I waited a few minutes for the shuttle with the ramp to arrive. It was a beautiful day, so I took the opportunity to soak up the sun. A red Nissan Altima was waiting for me. It had hand controls and a spinner knob.

Getting a rental car with viable hand controls was nearly impossible not so long ago. I sat in the driver's seat, took my wheelchair apart, and carefully placed the wheels over my body onto the front seat floor. Then, I collapsed the body of my chair and pulled it over my body onto the passenger seat. Driving down the road toward the condo, I felt my body relax immediately, a huge smile forming.

Full of joy, I was brave and listened to the messages I received, and here I was! I was on my first solo vacation. It was exhilarating! I got to the condo, pulled some clean clothes from my suitcase, and showered to get rid of the airplane. I made a list of things I needed at the grocery store and made the 15-minute drive to the nearest reasonably priced grocery store to pick up the essentials, knowing I'd return to the store a few times.

As I was unpacking groceries, there was a knock at the door. When I arrived, I noticed someone had patched a large area of the living room wall, but hadn't painted it. On the other side of the door was a painter, asking if he could come in and paint the patch. His energy was good, and I felt no threat, so I let him in. I learned he was from Virginia and had moved there recently to work for his uncle, who had a painting business.

We exchanged numbers, and he told me to call him if I needed anything while I was on the island. The first night, I relaxed and enjoyed the sounds of the crashing waves. The next day, I drove north to a little town called Paia. I was in a shop when I caught the eye of a handsome man with long black hair wet and sandy from surfing, his face decorated with a warm smile that spread to his eyes. I could see his soul.

He wore a beard of stubble, had beautiful dark brown skin, and had the most captivating brown eyes. We began talking, and when his hand touched mine, I felt the soul connection. We spent much of my trip together when he wasn't working. He took me out for a delicious dinner at the Sugar Mill after we had taken a stroll through the beautifully manicured grounds.

We watched the sunsets together while discussing anything and everything.

One day, he decided we would go on an adventure to the waterfalls. It's a bit of a hike for anyone to maneuver, let alone someone in a wheelchair. He told me with confidence that we could do it. We pulled up to the parking near the entrance to the dirt path leading to the waterfall and made our way down the path to the falls, slowly and methodically. It was hard work with all the turns and the uneven rocky pathway. Though he didn't complain, I could sense that he was exhausted by the time we got there.

We sat and watched the waterfalls, listening to the peaceful lull of the rush of water that magically calms the soul. We took pictures and talked, holding hands. Soon it started to rain. He moved quickly, gathering our things and preparing to push me back up the hills to get to the car. People asked if they could help as he pushed through the mud. He thanked each one and kept on.

We finally got to the top, taking refuge under the awning. Once the rain let up a little, we dashed to the car. My wheels were caked with mud. He swiftly took his sweatshirt off, used it to clean my messy wheels, and loaded the wheelchair into the car. Am I in one of those romance movies women dream about? I felt so loved then and had only known him for a few days.

There is nothing like a man caring for you. The week continued with more magic. My heart was healing. Looking into his eyes, I knew real and complete soul-connected love. He was an angel, sent to teach me that I was enough just as I was. He taught me to truly love every inch of myself by loving every inch of me and made me feel beautiful.

I had a newfound confidence about my body and its true beauty and lost all desire to hide any part of me from him. He taught me that I am deserving of unconditional love and that I am a goddess. His name is Aurelio. Translated from Spanish, Aurelio means 'Golden'. I met the man surrounded by gold, and he forever changed me and my life. For that and him, I am truly grateful.

Bio

Amy I. King is a Certified Life Coach/owner of Your Phenomenal Life, LLC. She is the best-selling author of *Messy Wheels: Stories From Where I Sit* and contributing author of international bestsellers: *Inspirations: 101 Uplifting Stories for Daily Happiness, Manifestations: True Stories of Bringing the Imagined into Reality, The Grateful Soul: The Art and Practice of Gratitude, The Courageous Heart: Finding Strength in Difficult Times, Ordinary Oneness, Enduring Wis-*

dom, 365 Days of Self Love, Whispers from the Heart, Wisdom Keepers, and many more. When not writing, she enjoys improv classes, cardio drumming, music, movies, art, meditation, travel, and time spent with her chosen family.

Amy has overcome many challenges from which she draws wisdom to assist clients. Amy's greatest joy is using her experiences to help others move past their personal blocks and outdated beliefs to become empowered to live their dreams. Every challenge, she believes, is put before us to enable us to evolve and grow into the highest version of ourselves.

She builds relationships with clients based on trust and vulnerability. She welcomes the opportunity to help you transform your life!

Email her at Amy.kinglifecoaching@gmail.com.

Chapter 22

The Journey to Self-Actualization: Beyond Manifestation

By Nadia S. Krauss

I n the realm of personal development, the concept of the law of attraction has gained significant traction, with many advocating positive thinking as a means to manifest desires and achieve goals. My introduction to this idea came at a tender age, guided by my father's exploration of spirituality and personal growth in his fifties. At the age of 11, he handed me my first personal development book, *You Can If You Think You Can*, by Norman Vincent Peale, emphasizing the transformative power of thought.

His message was clear: one could shape one's reality by thinking in the right way, a notion rooted in the law of attraction. Little did he know that the subconscious, often harboring unresolved wounds, plays a crucial role in the manifestation process. Regardless of how positive one's thinking is, manifesting from a wounded subconscious might not yield the desired outcomes. My father lacked the tools to address these energetic blocks and past traumas, hindering him from creating the life he truly desired.

However, this early exposure set me on a path of exploration into quantum healing practices. Delving into modalities such as the Akashic records, morphogenetic fieldwork, and Soul Art journey vision quests, I began to unravel the intricate connection between self-actualization and the embodiment of soul gifts and talents.

Growing up, my parents consistently encouraged me to pursue the best life imaginable, instilling hope, optimism, and positive expectancy. Their openness to life fostered a belief in the power of manifestation from a young age. Yet, life's complexities revealed a flip side as my parents grappled with recurring challenges—primarily revolving around relationship and financial struggles.

The lesson became clear: life is more than just "thinking the right way." It involves tapping into our unique set of soul gifts, which serve as guides toward our divine potential. These gifts encapsulate our deepest desires and aspirations, defining our purpose in this lifetime. Simultaneously, they unveil negative karmic patterns, blocks, and restrictions that keep us ensnared in repetitive cycles.

In the pursuit of societal expectations and instant gratification, my parents, like many, fell prey to the belief that success equates to a predefined set of achievements—career milestones, financial stability, luxurious homes, and other status symbols. This conditioning created a disconnect between mind, body, heart, spirit, and soul, allowing ego-driven desires to dictate their narrative.

The constant pursuit of immediate satisfaction hindered the mastery of the alchemical process essential for transformation and creation. Always chasing the next shiny object, my parents missed the essence of inhabiting their bodies in alignment with their soul gifts.

Soul gifts, in their essence, propel us toward our soul desires and divine potential. They beckon us to embody our bodies in a balanced and aligned manner, urging us to cultivate intuition and to hear divine guidance. This journey of embodiment and alignment is the transformative process known as self-actualization.

As I embarked on my exploration of self-actualization beyond mere manifestation, I discovered the importance of delving into the depths of the subconscious. True transformation requires addressing wounds, releasing energetic blocks, and understanding the intricate dance between the conscious and subconscious mind.

The journey involves embracing the alchemy of the soul, where the integration of mind, body, and spirit harmonizes with the soul's desires. It requires patience, introspection, and a willingness to confront the shadows within. Through practices like the Akashic records and Soul Art therapy, I learned to navigate the terrain of my subconscious, uncovering the layers that held me back from realizing my full potential.

Self-actualization, I realized, is not about wishful thinking but a profound journey of inner exploration. It demands a conscious effort to align with one's soul gifts, acknowledge and heal past wounds, and cultivate a deep connection with the divine guidance within. This process goes beyond the surface level of manifestation, transcending the ego's desires and paving the way for a more profound, authentic existence.

In conclusion, my journey from early exposure to the law of attraction to the profound realization of self-actualization has been transformative. It's a journey that continues to unfold, inviting me to explore the depths of my being and embrace the divine potential that resides within. Beyond the allure of instant gratification, I've come to understand that true fulfillment comes from aligning with the wisdom of the soul and navigating the intricate dance between manifestation and self-actualization.

Bio

Nadia S. Krauss, Author of *The Magic of Transformation: Igniting & Manifesting Your Soul Desires*, is a dedicated advocate for Soul Health and Divine self-expression. Her passion comes to life as she guides clients through the transformative Soul Realignment Power Retrieval Process.

In a pivotal moment, faced with the decline of True Love and labeled a "loser" by her ex-business partner, Nadia and her husband embarked on a courageous journey. They made the daring decision to sell all their possessions and work on a cruise ship for two years before relocating from Germany to the United States and then to Canada.

This bold move not only revitalized their marriage but also laid the foundation for a business centered on self-love leadership.

As the visionary founder of Soul Health Mentor & Company, the creator of the Soul Health Mentor Podcast, and a skilled facilitator of the Soul Realignment Power Retrieval Process, Nadia invites you to explore the profound link between your body, mind, heart, emotion, and Soul's medicine. Through regular heart space connection and all-encompassing health and wellness talks, she inspires and empowers you to manifest the dreams your soul holds for you, utilizing your spiritual gifts.

Nadia's journey is a testament to the transformative power of embracing one's authenticity and navigating life's challenges with resilience and self-love.

Website: https://nadiakrauss.com

Email: nadia@happywholesomelife.com

Chapter 23

Overcoming Limits

By Nina Kropp

L imits are put on us from an early age. They help to keep us safe, but when they are applied without maturity or good intentions, healthy growth *cannot* take place. They become exactly that: *limits*! They are no longer guidelines but other people's beliefs limiting us from becoming our best self and doing what we truly desire. We are told we can't do that, you shouldn't do that, or girls can't do that. There are so many limiting beliefs that society, our family, and friends have imposed on us. Often, these limits come as labels: you're bipolar, you're depressed, you have ADHD, you are intense, or you don't have family support; you can't do that!

The anger and fighting between my mother and step-father were unsurmountable! It was so bad that I couldn't take it and decided that I would live with my birth father, whom I visited at Christmas and during the summers. This was probably my first experience with overcoming limits. At age 14, I realized that this environment would be the death of my soul and dreams, so I packed extra clothes one summer and asked to stay with my father and his new wife. If this move had not worked, I was going to run away.

My high school boyfriend of four years was abusive physically and mentally. I knew no different. I watched my mom and stepfather have a violent and explosive relationship, so I figured that was what love is. It started with him pinching the inside of my thighs to get me to be quiet. The relationship culminated in an underground parking lot after I got off work. He grabbed me and bit my ear as I struggled to get away. He slammed my face on the asphalt and told me that if he couldn't have me, nobody would. I was trying to break up with him again. He held me in a chokehold and got me in the truck. He then proceeded to tell me that he was going to kill me. I was able to break free when he started to cry. I had to lie, comfort him, and say it was okay and that we would be okay.

I had to have the strength to go back to school and finish my finals or lose my first semester of college. He, of course, knew my schedule because he kept close tabs on my whereabouts. I thought, I'm doing this, and you're not taking my education away! Bring it on! That was my second test at age 19 of trying to break out of limits set by others.

I jumped out of the frying pan right into the fire. After breaking free from this abusive relationship, I started dating a sergeant of a police department who was 13 years older than me. Everyone told me that it wouldn't work because of the age difference, so I wanted to prove them wrong, so I married him. This was not the best choice, but I was determined *not* to let people influence my decisions.

I wanted to go to grad school to become a guidance counselor, but my husband told me I couldn't do that. He tried to say that he didn't feel safe with me going to school at night, so I told him to come and pick me up. The reality was that this would've surpassed his level in college. I went to grad school without his approval.

This created discord, and although I only had three classes left to finish my master's degree, I couldn't handle the tension at home, so I decided to leave. Now, here's where my memory is a little foggy, and it's probably because I have tried to put those people who have placed limits on me by putting me down and telling me I can't do something in the farthest depths of my memory. I was told by many people that there's no way you can become a principal. What did I do? I enrolled in grad school and started all over again with a different master's degree in educational leadership.

I come from a time when children were seen and not heard. In a way, those are the first limits that were put on me. Do as I say because I'm the parent! Although their choices may not have been the most logical decisions, I do have to say that I know my parents did the best they could at the time; not having guidance themselves as children, they were figuring it out. My mom packed up our house in trash bags every six months, leaving and coming back. Even as a small child, I knew this was bad.

The reason I tell you this is because this is the first conditioning I had that you go with the flow, and even though your instincts are telling you otherwise, you may not voice or act on them! You may not follow your dreams if they are going to make others sad or make them feel bad about themselves. I do have to brag that I was the first person in my family to go to college and graduate! I have a BA and a master's degree.

I've been in several abusive relationships, and those put limiting beliefs on me. You can't make it without me! Who else is going to love you? You are not lovable! If you've ever been in any type of abusive relationship, the manipulation and head games make you doubt yourself. They flip the script and make you feel crazy. Gaslighting you, making you doubt how you're thinking and feeling. They are masters in separating you from your wants, desires, and dreams. They even disconnect you from your relationships with family and friends.

It is not surprising that my sergeant husband was controlling. I didn't have confidence or self-esteem yet, but that grew over the next 13 years. I realized that people probably got tired of me complaining about my horrible, unfulfilling marriage, so I decided to leave. I always felt alone in our relationship, so I thought I would rather be alone than in this toxic environment. I mustered up the courage to believe in myself and start all over again at age 32. Unfortunately, it would take me another 25 years before I could truly manifest the life that I wanted and deserved.

I am a work in progress, and I catch myself sometimes reverting to old behaviors that don't serve me anymore. I finally realize how limiting beliefs held me back. I was staying in past trauma and letting it guide my future. I would often avoid my triggers because they were so earth-shattering that I didn't want to feel that pain ever again.

I now realize that my triggers are unhealed trauma. If I want to live a healthier and happier life, I must address them and not avoid them. I live in the present and not the past now. This helps me to let go of my old ways of coping by not always having to be a fighter. I am no longer the victim but a warrior who can do whatever she sets her mind to.

Thoughts are extremely powerful. For example, if you stub your toe, cuss, spill coffee on yourself and then *think* you're going to have an awful day, then you are going to have a terrible day! I guarantee that your day will not change when you are putting out that negative energy. That is exactly what you're getting back. You are manifesting it!

Think of one of those days when you're in the zone. Everything is going your way. It seems that way because *you* are open to the possibilities that the world is offering you. We often hold ourselves back. We tell ourselves that we can't or shouldn't do something. Maybe this stems from those limits others have been putting on us? Whatever it is, I truly believe and have experienced the power of manifesting the life you truly want and deserve.

We all have *magic* within us. If we recognize internally that the limitations we put on ourselves are not chains that bind us, then we can live our best lives. It is a mindset when you start believing in yourself; nothing can hold you back! The power of the mind is limitless, and so are you!

Bio

Nina Kropp exudes positivity and is living her best life despite her struggles with depression for 40 years. She is a former teacher, VP, principal, high school counselor, administrator in a women's correctional facility, juvenile sex offender counselor and abuse survivor.

Feel free to contact her at NinaKropp@icloud.com.

Chapter 24

The Lovelight Connection

By Colleen Lovelight

I felt the bumper of the massive Pontiac sedan pressed against the back of my head as it vibrated in rhythm with every screech of the tires, pushing my tiny seven-year-old body down the street. As if to fulfill a prophecy, I ignored my gut feeling to not cross our quiet street.

I should have been seriously injured. But when the car stopped, I jumped up like being jolted out of a dream into extreme chaos. Everything was happening all at once. A woman grabbed me by my shoulders and yelled, "Little girl, are you okay?" The man driving the sedan screamed in a different language while other people shouted, "Call the police!"

I ran two doors down, up three flights of stairs, and hid in my bedroom. My parents weren't home, and I was terrified. I had no recollection of being hit from the side, thrown in the air, and landing on my bum in front of the car. As people witnessed this horrific accident, I was somewhere else. It was unclear for years to come, but I had a vague recollection and called it "the in-between."

Dad was due to return home from a trip that day, and it wasn't uncommon for my mother to leave me on my own. Mom took my younger brother grocery shopping, leaving me to play outside with neighborhood kids. The downstairs neighbors knew I was hiding in my room and called to me to wait with them until one of my parents came home.

Dad arrived home first and immediately took me to the ER. Doctors and nurses poked, prodded, and kept asking if I had pain. After a full check-up with x-rays, *nothing was wrong*! I did not have a bruise, a scratch, or any pain! They told Dad I was very lucky.

This life-changing event in 1972 placed me on a trajectory of trauma, setting the tone for the rest of my childhood.

My father blamed my mother for putting me at risk, and they split up within a week. He made a life-altering decision for our family. He wanted to marry my mother's cousin, Lori. (Months before their split, we would visit Lori and her husband, Z. The situation made me feel uncomfortable and unsafe. I witnessed Z abusing Lori and other things that didn't make sense in my seven-year-old brain until days after my accident.) When Dad made his announcement to my mother, he was holding a gun in his hand, telling her that if she tried to take "his kids," he'd kill her.

And just like that, Mom vanished into the night. Throughout my life, I learned she was a voiceless victim. My brother and I went to bed one night with my mother tucking us in and awoke the next morning to Cousin Lori coming out of our parent's bedroom. Her daughter was there too. Abandoned by my mother, a new family of secrets was formed overnight. I was shattered by her disappearance. But no one knew because I remained stoic, and never cried.

Months went by before we finally got to see Mom, but it was not what I had hoped. She was living with Z, and just as he had done with Lori, he was abusing my voiceless mother. I witnessed this nightmare on numerous visits. Another secret I was to keep. When my mother got herself out of that abusive relationship, she went into another for the next 25 years. I wanted to save her, but this painful lesson of acceptance was that I could not save her from herself.

Lori was to raise my brother and me. She was nice, at first, but it only took about a month for that to change. My three-year-old brother and I endured consistent and horrific mental, emotional, and physical abuse from her while my father worked. Lori threatened me to never tell anyone, or she would make our lives worse by taking it out on my brother and father.

We lived in a home that was full of violence, drugs, and alcoholism. Even after my youngest sister was born, Lori and Dad continued the wild parties and violent arguments while drunk or high. They put on the charade of a happy family for extended family, the church community, and our neighborhood. I did my best to protect my three younger siblings while being subjected to mental, emotional, and physical abuse. I raised my baby sister, shopped, did laundry, cooked meals, and constantly babysat. I lived in fear for my life and the lives of my brother and mother for years.

I refer to my childhood as walking among a sea of the insane and where my warrior training commenced. I learned how to survive by reading energy and predicting outcomes. It didn't take long for me to construct my suit of armor adorned with rage and fearlessness so I could feel powerful and safe. I promised myself I would never be a voiceless victim like my mother. As a teenager, I engaged in physical warfare with Lori or anyone in the streets of the not-so-safe neighborhood where we lived.

My warrior training was useful in my career, where I needed to be aggressive to succeed among the hierarchy of men. Adulthood served plenty more lessons through repeated patterns, financial challenges, and the heartbreaking experiences of emotional abandonment that included two failed marriages. However, I was able to experience profound love with my three children. Their love opened my heart, which had been closed off for so long and provided the most valuable education on my self-love mission.

In my 30s, I embarked upon a self-exploration, starting with my natural ability to read energy and predict outcomes to help others. I took psychic development classes, became Reiki certified, and provided assistance to family, friends, and the executive team I worked with. While the accuracy of the information I offered sometimes frightened people, I found it to be fun. I became more intrigued and invested energy into other ways to expand myself. I incorporated energy healing sessions, therapy, and yoga. I read many self-development and metaphysical books.

This process took years to peel back layers of protection and required that I allow myself to be vulnerable through shadow work, acceptance, forgiveness, and sitting with my inner child to appreciate her strength. I utilized all of life's challenges to understand myself intimately. Life delivers these opportunities to us consistently so we can understand and expand into self-acceptance and self-love.

Through this work, "the in-between" was fully revealed. My body was placed in suspended animation while my consciousness left this 3D world. I felt the peaceful, warm, and loving presence of the divine. I blended into and became one with this immense energy. This near-death experience was where my auspicious and sacred agreement was formulated. I was to be indoctrinated by the ego, learn how it worked, understand it deeply, and remain separate from the divine until I awakened to self-love through healing.

I resurrected as an empowered thriver. I fell in love with my inner divine feminine, a part of myself that I was not familiar with. This newly formed bond allowed me to remove my armor and evolve from unhealthy rage to love. I realized that my human experience brought me to a level of frequency for others who needed my specific resonance in support of their healing and awakening to self-love.

The divine feminine beckoned from the depths of my soul to facilitate her work. I pursued an education in alternative holistic healing, opened a wellness center, and successfully created a divine feminine community of healers for six years. COVID closed the center to free up my time from day-to-day management, creating space for me to support more women individually and in groups.

I have been honored to witness the awakening of thousands of awe-inspiring women on their evolutionary process to self-love as they heal and ignite their inner lovelight through divine feminine empowerment. Their lovelight shines into the darkness so others can find their own.

The divine feminine may have been dormant, but I assure you, we are awake. We have fearlessly empowered ourselves, wielding love. We are the new paradigm here to expand consciousness to oneness. As we ignite the world from our inner lovelight, we disintegrate the old paradigm belief system of the ego.

Bio

Colleen Kutcher Ofsanik, CNHP, RMT, CYT, CST, Naturopathic Practitioner, is a spiritual advisor, educator, intuitive healer, and divine feminine community creator.

Colleen has successfully provided education and facilitated healing for thousands of clients on their evolutionary process to self-love. Her lovelight shines brightest when women empower themselves in this auspicious work through private sessions and sacred gatherings.

Her deepest lovelight connections are her children and grandchildren, who reflect the meaning of true love.

The Lovelight Connection

lovelighthc.com

Chapter 25

Signposts to Purpose

By Joe McMonagle

"Stop talking!" I mumbled during an online meeting, frustrated it was running past its scheduled end time. Glancing at the microphone icon on the screen, I panicked when I realized it was on. Having worked at this company for twenty years, I realized I remained in my job mainly to pay my bills. It didn't give me a sense of purpose. I yearned for divine guidance to illuminate the path where I belonged. Have you ever felt trapped in a job like I did?

But let's backtrack. This job was only one segment on the meandering path I traveled in search of my purpose. Some might have called it chaotic. Reflecting on it, I want to share the five signposts that were turning points and opportunities for change.

Signpost 1: The Stranger

I was pursuing my Master's degree in engineering when a friend approached me with a request. Host his friend for a few days. The prospect of entertaining a stranger terrified me. I wasn't someone who took risks. Because I always felt different throughout childhood, I tried to blend into the background. My dislike of sports further isolated me, resulting in bullying and the gradual erosion of my self-esteem. A skewed understanding of God as a judge compounded my struggle. My friend's request became my first signpost. I would have declined had I not recalled my faith's instruction to welcome the stranger.

One night, my guest introduced me to the Catholic Charismatic Renewal, which celebrates their faith through song, prayer, and praise in tongues. Intrigued, I attended one of their meetings and witnessed people excited about their faith and convinced of God's unconditional love. Although their belief didn't make sense, I yearned for their experience and decided to join.

Over the next nine months, I underwent a renewal. Not only did I begin to feel God's love, but I also discovered a new form of prayer: chatting with God. I had never thought prayer could be anything but formulaic. With this renewal came a feeling of joy I had never known. If anyone had come by my office during those months, they would have heard me enthusiastically belting out songs by Amy Grant, a Christian singer, and concluded I'd lost my mind. Out of my transformation grew a desire for others to experience the same.

Signpost 2: The Call

With that desire came a call to the priesthood, the next signpost. I felt excited about putting my passion into action as a priest. However, my excitement waned when I began applying to the diocesan seminary. Sitting in the chapel building on campus, I felt my head swirling with doubts. Had I misread the signpost? Sharing my confusion with God, I pleaded, "Could you send someone to me with whom I could talk?"

Minutes later, two friends walked in. My mouth dropped open when they told me they were returning from a vocational retreat sponsored by the Paulist Fathers. God had heard my plea. I felt a spark ignite in my heart when they shared that this community of priests dedicated their lives to helping people find healing, connection, and meaning. The spark became a roaring fire when I discovered its founders emphasized the importance of each person following the guidance of the Holy Spirit wherever it might lead. That aligned with my own belief, fully resonating with me. Without hesitation, I applied, and they accepted me.

Through the ensuing formation years, I experienced tremendous growth. My bond with God strengthened through the study of theology and scripture. Therapy also played a pivotal role as emotional wounds began to heal, which resulted in me acknowledging my identity as a gay man. A bishop ordained me and my classmates at the end of my sixth year, and my purpose seemed clear.

Signpost 3: The Hiccup

I was on vacation from my assignment to my second parish when I experienced a hiccup with my purpose. On the second day, an unexpected desire for an intimate relationship surfaced. Despite my attempts to ignore it, the feeling kept returning, as hiccups often do. This new signpost took the form of two questions: Is my desire so vital I must leave the priesthood? Or can I set it aside and remain a celibate priest? Intuitively, I knew I needed time away to consider them. God sent signs confirming this when I found an apartment and a job in the software industry within two weeks of leaving. This job was similar to the one I mentioned at the beginning of my article.

Unfortunately, those questions led to three more. How could I leave a community I loved and with whom I had made a lifetime commitment? Could I even find someone to date? If I didn't return, what about my call to serve, which was as strong as ever? Guilt and fear weighed heavily on me. Months into the leave, I met the man to whom I'd give my heart and marry five years later. Having decided not to return to the priesthood, I was back to square one, wondering about my purpose.

Signpost 4: The Search

Thus, the search for my purpose resumed. I considered options like volunteering or working in the non-profit sector. Both felt wrong. At a therapeutic retreat, an offhand remark became the next signpost: You could be a therapist. An online search led me to a degree program with a spiritual emphasis. Not only was the university ten minutes away, but my boss supported a flexible work schedule. I knew God played a role there.

Midway through my final year, while seeing clients as a therapist trainee, a stark realization hit me. My classmates showed a passion for this work I lacked. I realized this was not my path, but I still decided to complete the degree. I must admit that by then,

I was frustrated. I'd pursued four professions but had yet to find my life's purpose. "Come on, God," I complained. Thirteen more years went by before the next signpost appeared.

Signpost 5: The Pink Slip

Getting laid off was a blow. I felt angry and betrayed. However, unlike me, God and my other divine advisors saw this as an opportunity. Aware I had diligently saved for retirement, a few years away, they suggested I create a new profession. My response: "Are you crazy? You want me to make something up?" Their persistent encouragement, almost bordering on harassment, prompted me to ask how, albeit reluctantly. They advised me to look for moments of passion.

Three stood out. The first took me back to graduate school and my desire for others to experience God's love as I did. The second occurred at the counseling center while a therapist trainee. In a conversation with a staff member, I felt my passion bubble over as I shared my desire with her. The therapeutic retreat revealed the third moment when its founder expressed her belief that I had the qualities of a spiritual healer.

Today

My identity as a spirit healer is still evolving. At its core is my belief that each person must forge a path that resonates with them, regardless of whether they believe in a divine entity. My commitment to helping others heal brokenness, rediscover their blessedness, and uncover their purpose stems from this belief. A website, monthly blogs, and a spiritual fantasy, which is currently in development, are the manifestations of that commitment.

Looking back, I'm grateful for the twists and turns of my meandering path. Each signpost marked a crucial juncture, built upon what came before. Will there be more signposts? Of course. These unknown moments will also likely come with doubt and fear. But my divine advisors encourage me to embrace the unknown and be open to the miracles ahead.

Back to your search for purpose. If you're already living it, congratulations. Enjoy it. If not, try to believe your life is building towards it. Search within and identify your passion; that's the magic. Inevitably, magic manifests.

Bio

Joe McMonagle is a devoted spirit healer, guiding individuals along their life journey in pursuit of healing, connection to their divine essence, and discovery of their purpose. With a diverse educational background, Joe holds a Bachelor of Architectural Engineering, a Master of Divinity, and a Master of Arts in Counseling Psychology. His professional journey spans 12 years as a religious seminarian/priest and 26 years in the software industry. Alongside his career, Joe remains steadfast in his commitment to spiritual growth, exploring belief systems and healing practices. Influenced by esteemed teachers like Denise Linn, Liz Dawn, Terry Bowen, Neale Donald Walsh, Dougall Fraser, and Kyle Gray, Joe continues to expand his knowledge. Discover more about Joe's work on his website, www.joemcmonaglehsp.com. Connect with him through that website or via email at jmcmonaglehsp@gmail.com.

Chapter 26

A Curious Invitation

By Sally Malik

Back in the cavemen's days, belonging was critical to survival. If we weren't a part of the tribe, if we were left out and alone, this left us vulnerable to getting eaten or worse, so it was really important that we constantly evaluated, "Am I good enough to be in this tribe? Am I pulling my weight? Am I looking like the other people that are around me?" because it was a survival technique.

Fast-forward this to today, and we're constantly evaluating ourselves as right, or wrong, or good, or bad in an effort to belong.

Again, while long ago, this brain function kept us safe, in today's world, constantly looking around and feeling inferior makes us feel more alone.

What helps instead? I work with clients to accept emotions and cope with them instead. This means that we need to actively work to dispel the myth that we are always meant to be happy and instead help ourselves to gain the tools we need to manage life's ups and downs.

This also means that we have a responsibility to be curious about our emotions rather than punitive, critical, or judgmental about them. When we notice ourselves getting tense or angry, or sad, or slamming a door, don't automatically rush into berating your-self—instead, get curious about what's behind that behavior.

We always look at behaviors as a means of communicating an emotion. Let's get curious about what it is that our emotions are communicating via our behaviors. Notice whether you have activated your inner critic with your emotions. Then, see if you can pull apart the message embedded in that emotion.

As an example, I wanted to share a parable with you.

If you know me, you know that I love animals. You also know that I think we learn so much from them. This parable does a great job of illustrating that.

There was an old man sitting on a park bench. A songbird landed in a nearby tree and began to sing. The old man listened joyfully. A short time passed, and the old man noticed a hawk circling high in the sky. He thought to himself, "Oh, no. What if that hawk spots that little songbird?" As the hawk soared closer and closer, the old man got more and more nervous. He hung on to each moment in hopes that the hawk would fly off in a different direction. The little bird continued to sing. Soon, the hawk was very near, and the old man could no longer sit and wait. He yelled at the little bird, "Fly away, little bird." The little bird was startled and flew straight towards the hawk. The hawk grabbed the bird, flew to a nearby tree and had his afternoon snack.

This little parable is a reminder of what we often do when we confront a struggle. If the little old man had not intervened, the little bird would likely have sensed the hawk, stopped singing and never been noticed by the hawk. Or, the hawk would have seen the bird anyway and had his afternoon meal anyway. Then, why do we feel like we need to intervene?

It is because we feel responsible.

What does it mean when we feel responsible? Being responsible is an act of self-consciousness. "I feel like I must do something for this to occur or not to occur." Self-consciousness is the result of a belief that there is an I and there is a you. It is the nature of human beings. Self-consciousness was created by the ego-mind, and we became dependent on it for our answers. It was the old man's ego-mind that told him to shout out at the little bird.

And, it was the ego-mind that later told him, "Maybe you shouldn't have done that."

It is the fear of not being responsible enough that brings on our suffering. It is the strength of the fearful emotion that gives us a sense of self. As long as there is a me that feels responsible for solving the problem, then I will maintain my sense of being a me.

With this concept in mind, our worries are a state of mind because all events are neutral. They only become a problem when our ego-mind tells us that it is. Then, out of a sense of responsibility, we scramble to solve the problem, using tremendous amounts of energy while resisting the experience and creating great emotional suffering.

Avoiding this suffering is not a realistic option. We can, however, begin to be aware of what is going on in our minds. We can notice that we have the choice to engage with our thoughts or to just watch them as the silent witness. One invitation I have to offer is to accept and allow. This doesn't seem reasonable to the ego-mind, but it is the ego-mind that interprets life events as difficult. Maybe, by simply noticing and allowing, we find peace and guidance.

It may also be an opportunity for self-compassion and kindness—concepts we don't readily embrace.

Let's better understand self-compassion and kindness with another lesson from animals.

Last night, I went to a dinner party with some friends and some people I did not know. Several of the guests brought dogs to the party, and one woman brought a dog we'll call "scared dog." Scared dog was the smallest of the dogs and would bark at everything—the other dogs, food, new people, and people walking around. The owner began to get tired of this and embarrassed. She started trying to control scared dog by yelling "Hey!" at him. Scared dog would freeze for a moment and then go on barking again.

Eventually, the owner started getting more and more frustrated and started yelling, "Shut up!" and even yanking on his leash to try to get him to stop.

I decided to go over to scared dog when he was barking and started to pet him, reassure him, and tell him, "Everything is okay."

Scared dog would start to calm down and would actually stop barking. I kept going over to scared dog every time he would bark and continue to comfort him. He would relax and stop barking.

Eventually, the owner started to catch on. She saw that comforting and being kind to scared dog actually worked and got the result she was looking for in the first place. By the end of the party, she too would pet him and tell him, "It is okay," and sure enough, scared dog would relax and be okay.

How often do we treat our own inner scared dog this way? How often do we tell ourselves we shouldn't be scared? Or get angry with ourselves for feeling a certain way?

The point isn't really that being kind to ourselves (and dogs) is the "right" thing; it's that being kind actually works to lower our distress. Beating ourselves up and trying to control how our distress simply backfires.

Self-love is not really a woo-woo weird spiritual thing. It's what our biology needs in times of distress.

And yet, we are conditioned to believe beating ourselves up is the only option, the "right" thing to do.

It isn't. We can always choose to be kind to ourselves, not because we "should" but because it simply helps.

My final invitation to you, after sharing the story of this beautiful, scared dog: What does your inner scared dog ask of you in being kind? How can we be curious instead of berating our needs in moments of distress? Curiosity in place of criticism opens the door for self-compassion, kindness to ourselves, and self-love. It is under these conditions that our version of our best selves begins to flourish.

Bio

Sally Malik is a licensed clinical psychologist, Reiki Master/Teacher, crystal healer, animal communicator, LWISSD certified psychic medium, Yoga Alliance registered yoga instructor, certified meditation teacher, and ordained interfaith minister. She offers holistically oriented emotional healing to people and animals, along with intuitive readings.

Sally is currently attaining advanced certifications and training with renowned spiritual teachers and is deeply passionate about living a whole, fulfilled life in harmony with what brings us joy and aligns with our higher soul purpose. Sally is also the author of the book *All Is Love: The Pet Solution*, which celebrates our loving connection with animals and is a regular contributor to several publications as well as host of her podcast, *Beyond the Couch*.

Her goal is to help you connect with your higher self, departed loved ones, and animals energetically, spiritually, and emotionally to live the connected life you celebrate every day. Website: www.sallymalik.com, email: sallymalikmedium@gmail.com.

Chapter 27

Let Sparks Fly

By Janine Nelson

As a young girl, I instinctively knew everything happens for a reason. When my attitude was positive, good things occurred. If I saw nice-looking flowers, I would draw them. Days later, we had flowers in the house. I had a strong passion for horses. A week later, I began taking riding lessons. Everything happens for a reason.

I discovered my magic didn't work when I was angry or contentious. That's when I understood the connection. Positive mental images create my positive world. This evolved into magic. Everyone holds a bright spark of magic and creativity. It's time to use it.

Now, I apply magic to achieve goals by writing them down and sending them to the universe. I employ magic to heal friends and family. I have even used my magic to manifest money to cover bills. When I need a boost of confidence or to amplify my creativity, I mentally focus and spark my magic with a deep breath.

Most of us have performed magic at some point in time. Have you guessed what that might be? Consider your birthday or a celebration when there was a delicious cake or cupcake with candles. Remember those tiny, colorful candles with vivid flames on your cake? The voice behind you says, "Make a wish, then blow out your candles." With fine-tuned focus, you closed your eyes, filled your lungs with air, and blew out the candles. Blowing out those flames created smoke. The smoke carried your wish up and out into the universe. This austere process taught us how magic could make our dreams come true. This is the first way we learn to attain desires and is the simplest.

Do you remember it? Did you realize deep in your soul that your wish would come true? That whole process creates a connection to the goddess, the gods, and the universe, asking them for help. I still feel those sparks whenever I work magic and connect with the universe.

What if you decided to manifest something into your life, but it doesn't fulfill your highest purpose? In that case, the universe gently or acrimoniously shows you the better way. At times, it has been quite brutal with me. The resistance felt as if I had hit a brick wall. That wall was a message telling me to try again. I left the predetermined path of my life. I thought I knew better than the gods. The more I made careless attempts to keep going, the more bricks I encountered. My internal sparks began to diminish. I felt connections with the universe dwindling. Thankfully, that was only temporary.

Looking back, I admit that the goddess, spirit guides, and divine council worked frantically to usher me back to the right path. When I didn't act fast enough, a proverbial two-by-four ushered me back onto the proper road. Those two-by-fours are persuasive, but the pain imposed is the lesson learned, hopefully not repeated.

Re-connecting to the universe takes sweat equity through meditation, practice, and journaling. As your internal spark reignites and connections are established, there may be a tingle in your arms or legs. Others may hear a hum deep in their soul, while some may see signs all around. I feel sparks flying around me when I have made my spiritual connections.

Have you ever noticed that signs of spiritual connections are all around us? Seeing the patterns in which the universe communicates with us is fascinating. Animals and insects are great messengers of those signs. My favorites are dogs, crows, and dragonflies. When dragonflies appear, they symbolize change, transformations, and adaptability. Some symbolic meanings attributed to crows include magic, flexibility, adaptability, transformation, and destiny. Dogs are the symbols of loyalty, protection, perseverance, and playfulness. When I get serious, the dog is ready to make me laugh.

I have performed a variety of magical techniques to manifest dreams and pursuits. Some of my approaches are elegant, simple, and fun, while others can be jumbled and chaotic. When one method doesn't work, it's important to try another.

Working with one or more of the four elements assists me in communicating with the universe and obtaining my goals. Air, fire, earth, and water guide my magical process and help focus my intentions. I use different techniques for different purposes. Whatever your chosen method, you want the best outcome for your higher good. When I talk about "you're higher good," I'm referring to the idea that your life has a greater purpose or meaning beyond your desires and needs. Ultimately, your higher good is about living a personally fulfilling life that contributes to the greater good of all.

Be cautious when working your magic under stress or dire need because it may not work. It may even backfire. Step back, reflect, breathe, and focus to make your magic spark.

Your vision should be clear and concise. Don't muddle your goal or desire with extraneous goop. Don't add too much detail that the universe can't help. Do you want a 2024 Golden Tesla with extra features or an eco-friendly, operational, reliable car?

Once you've identified and clarified your goal, it's time to send it up to the divine and out to the cosmos. If you are working on significant long-range goals, they may take time and extra work. Identify and break down your goal into manageable tasks. This will help your manifestation process.

I like to incorporate surrounding energies and elements as aids in accomplishing my objectives. One of my favorite ways to manifest desires is by writing them on paper and burning them. I may add candles incorporating air, fire, and earth elements. Each element is a powerful spark that awakens my magic. So, let's grab paper and a candle and let the sparks fly.

You can choose any candle color, but let's keep it simple and use white. White is a universal color and denotes protection and new beginnings.

Writing my question, goal, or wish as a mantra is a creative way of using the element of air. Keep it simple, and make it rhyme. Rhyming helps you remember and is pleasant to the goddess and the universe. Place your candle on a plate or in a holder. Have a dish nearby to catch your burning paper.

As I light the candle, I begin repeating the mantra aloud. Recently, I had a decision to make. I wrote out my question, "Am I ready for another dog? I await your signs to continue on." When I was ready, I lit the paper from the candle flame and watched as it burned gently in the dish.

After the paper burned out, I focused on the candle flame as it flickered and changed shape. Flames are a unique way to determine if your process is working. If the candle's flame is large, it indicates confidence in your work, whereas a small flame indicates a lack of energy. You want a steady candle flame showing all is going well. When I saw a large, steady candle flame, I knew the sign I requested would soon show itself. So now what?

As the candle burns out, I use this time to write down my question or desire and the magical process used. This informs future work and whether my question was answered.

The universe is a mystical, powerful force. You can manifest your dreams and wishes once you acknowledge your spiritual connections. While the universe helped deliver most of my wishes and complete my goals, it provided better opportunities and directions when some dreams were not in my best interest.

Manifesting is a powerful tool that can help us improve our lives and bring us closer to the universe. I feel a sense of magic and wonder when sparks fly around me. It's essential to trust in the power of manifestation and allow your magic to work for you. So, go ahead and let your sparks fly. Enjoy the journey and what the universe has in store for you.

Bio

Janine Nelson has been a project manager, social media and marketing consultant, spirit worker, and rescues dogs. She earned her Bachelor of Science in Marketing from Barry University. Based on her intuition, she moved from Florida to California. Her positive attitude and magical sense helped her overcome difficult times after the move. She was hired as a marketing generalist for a large corporation, where she used her creative abilities to develop materials for company products. She gradually moved into a new role as a project manager after earning a project manager certification. Recently, her journey evolved as she retired to focus on photography and dogs. Janine volunteers for a local non-profit canine rescue, fostering puppies and senior dogs. She has been a "foster-fail" parent three times. Her most recent adoption, a Great Pyrenees named Oso, keeps her on her toes, both physically and mentally. You may contact Janine at jnelsoncreativeca@gmail.com.

Chapter 28

An Unexpected Gift

By Rosanne Norris

I had no intention of getting a dog, but Fritz was a gift that could not be denied.

As I sat in meditation on a cold January morning in 2020, a dog popped into my awareness. It quickly flashed in and out of my mind's eye, but I was sure it looked like a Schnauzer. Strange. Why would I see a Schnauzer? I never owned one or knew anyone who did. I was a regular meditator, but I had never had a vision, although I know some people do. Still, I was surprised by this experience. I questioned whether I saw it at all. Did I make it up?

When I explained what had happened to my husband, he told me he had been researching dogs the day before, as he thought he might surprise me with a puppy for my birthday, which was not until June. He said he was intrigued by the Miniature Schnauzer.

How interesting.

I marveled at this connection, but wasn't all that surprised. I had read how our brains act as antennas, sending and receiving consciousness, and sharing information. Knowing this, the fact I had tapped into my husband's stream of consciousness, made sense to me. But why had we shared this information? There must be a reason.

We discussed the idea of having a dog, and dismissed it as not the right time.

Then I got curious.

We were traveling to visit family that day, so I decided to research Miniature Schnauzers. A local breeder's website came up, with six or seven puppies immediately available. Puppies are cute. It can't hurt to look, right?

As I scrolled through the faces of those cute puppies, I was drawn to the face of one little pup. The photo was less clear than the others, but I kept going back to look at that blurry photo. It wasn't until the third or fourth look that I realized it was available on the exact day my son had passed two years prior.

I was stunned. How could this be? Was this a coincidence? Or something more?

Oxford Dictionary states a coincidence is "a remarkable concurrence of events or circumstances without apparent causal connection." Merriam-Webster says a coincidence is "the occurrence of events that happen at the same time by accident, but seem to have a connection."

I felt there was a connection.

In the late 20s or early 30s, Psychologist Carl Jung introduced the idea of synchronicity, in which two unrelated events or circumstances seem to have a connection. From this description, it seems Jung and Webster are saying the same thing. Science, however, explains these events in terms of probability rather than connection. For example, according to an article written by Robert Matthew for sciencefocus.com, there is "almost a 50:50 chance of at least two of the 23 players in any football match having the same birthday." Okay, this makes sense to me. Probability is how likely something happens. It's in the numbers.

However, I was not even looking for a dog, so I am not sure probability applies.

Jung believed the events that happen to us can hold a special meaning even though one thing did not cause the other to happen. I'm with Jung.

But back to Fritz's story.

I made a call to the breeder to arrange a visit for the next day. We arrived to find two litters of puppies squirming inside a corral in the breeder's living room. She pointed out the puppy, a three-pound runt among his boisterous peers. She said he had personality, and watching him, it was clear he was not intimidated by the others. I held him, unsure whether I wanted the responsibility of owning a dog. It had been nine years since we had to say goodbye to Ruby, our family beagle. I thanked the breeder and told her we would think about this monumental decision.

On the way home, we discussed the pros and cons of bringing a dog into our lives. We agreed it would be a game-changer. Every decision, from going out to dinner to going on vacation, would have to factor in a dog. Call it a coincidence or synchronicity, I couldn't shake the feeling he was meant to be ours, and quite possibly a gift from our son. And that was that. I called the breeder, and a few days later, we brought him home.

When this little three-pound runt walked into the house, he sat down, sniffed, and looked around like he knew the place. I had set up a bed inside a little corral like he was used to with his roommates. I was prepared for the sleepless nights I was sure were to happen like it does with most new puppies. But what happened surprised me. He slept contentedly from the very first night.

I named him Fritz. Miniature Schnauzer's are originally from Germany, but that is not why he bears that name. In one session, with a medium, I was told I would write a book, helped by a German writing guide with a long name that began with an F, which I would shorten. After waking up one night hearing strong German words, I shortened the long name to Fritz. And I honored my guide by naming my dog after him.

Spunky, sweet Fritz had us wrapped around his paw right from the beginning. He was smart and easy to housetrain, unlike our beagle, Ruby, who we had to send over the Rainbow Bridge in 2011. Ruby was a sweet dog, but quite stubborn, as Beagles are known to be, and not as bright as this new little pup seemed to be. But we loved her all the same.

A few weeks after Fritz came into our lives, I recalled a strange experience I had a number of months ago that now had me curious. One night, as I was falling asleep, I felt a depression behind me on the bed. At first, I was puzzled and thought my husband was getting in on the wrong side of the bed. Then I felt something walking around the bed, like an animal. I felt where my husband normally slept, but he wasn't there. The walking continued all over the bed. It was dark in the room, and I was a little afraid, so I didn't open my eyes. Then the thought came. Ruby? I immediately felt tingles along with a burst of love. I had never had an experience like this, and I wasn't sure what to make of it. As I drifted off to sleep, I sent gratitude to Ruby, and to Lee, thinking perhaps it was a sign that they are together.

I now believe it was more.

Reincarnation wasn't a concept I grew up with, but I was familiar with it now. I had read stories about very young children who knew things they couldn't have known about lives they had lived in the past, and when researched, turned out to be accurate. It didn't dawn on me that a pet might be able to do the same until I had another reading with a medium, who confirmed Fritz was a reincarnation of Ruby, who wanted to come back to help me heal. What a selfless act of love. There is no way I can prove this, but it rings true in my heart.

In the end, it doesn't matter to me whether it's a coincidence or synchronicity; Fritz and I have a connection that goes beyond pet and owner. When we look into each other's eyes, I feel an unbroken bond of love. He is my constant companion, and my soulmate. And he is a healing gift, sent in love, from my son in spirit, and that's all that matters. And for this, I am grateful.

Bio

Rosanne Norris embarked on a spiritual path, in 2018, after her thirty-year-old son, Lee, passed from an unexpected, accidental carbon monoxide poisoning. She is an affiliate leader and caring listener for a peer-to-peer based, international, non-profit organization called Helping Parents Heal, whose mission is to help parents after the loss of a child.

Rosanne is the author of the book *beLEEve: a Journey of Loss, Healing, and Hope* (2020) and a contributor to three anthologies: *Ordinary Oneness: The Simplicity of Everyday Love, Grace and Hope* (2021), *Gathering at the Doorway, An Anthology of Signs, Visits, and Messages from the Afterlife* (2022), and *Ignite Your Inner Fire* (2023). Rosanne was also featured in the award-winning documentary, *Rinaldi*, the story of Brazilian trans-communication researcher, Sonia Rinaldi, who for over thirty years has brought through images and voices from deceased loved ones.

Additionally, Rosanne is a Reiki Master, and a certified grief educator, trained by the world-renowned David Kessler.

Rosanne is working on future writing projects. Her other interests include reading spiritual books, podcasts, cooking, spending time with family, especially her grandchildren, and being with her beloved dog, Fritz.

She can be reached at rmnorris457@gmail.com.

Chapter 29

Divine Awakening

By Sylvie Robert

N estled deep inside each of us is the power to heal and to remember who we truly are! All my life, I felt supported by spirit. Against all odds, I healed myself many times over! When it is meant to be, at the perfect divine timing, you will bloom unexpectedly, and your heart will open wide! No need to work hard to attain it. Your heart will open wide at the right time for you and not before. Therefore, let's enjoy the ride and be ready to see miracles.

The universe knew who I was even before I found out! I want to bring you back to a very special time in my life, a moment with great impact. It was the moment I realized I was magic: the universe was going through my veins, I was rooted in the earth and connected to all life through love and light. It was also the moment

I knew that the universe had my back! I was in awe and still am when I recall that day.

Let's see what led to that moment. Back in my university days, I told my roommate that my best friend at that time was pregnant and would ask me to be the godmother of her child. My roommate laughed and asked me why I was so sure. I told her that my intuition was strong about it, and I believed in it. Then the phone rang, and my best friend asked me to come visit her because she had an important question to ask me. When I came back home, I told my roommate that my friend had asked me to be her child's godmother. My roommate's mouth opened wide. She was stunned! Being a godmother was the biggest honor someone could give me. I love children and always dreamed of becoming a mother.

I was on standby for the child's birth. My friend had asked me and others to be there by her side for the birth because her husband had left her during the pregnancy. I wouldn't have missed it for the world! One evening, she called me to tell me she was on her way to the hospital as her contractions were getting closer and stronger. We all immediately went to be by her side. Once I arrived, the doctors told us that it was just Braxton Hicks contractions and that she wasn't truly in labor. My friend told us to go home to sleep as it could be a long time before she would give birth. Others left, but my intuition told me to stay with her that night. It was such a strong calling I stayed despite admonitions from others that I should leave.

Later that night, real labor started. I was so happy that I had heeded my intuition! I remember vividly what happened that night. I was sitting on a chair on her left side, holding her hand, thankful that she wasn't alone. Her grandmother had intended to be the one holding her hand for this momentous occasion, but it was clear that those who had gone home wouldn't make it back on time for the birth.

After pushing through the birth canal, this beautiful infant's head came out facing me. I was, therefore, the first person she had ever seen. I also saw great panic in the eyes of the doctor and nurses when they saw the umbilical cord wrapped twice around the baby's neck, causing its face to turn blue! The cord was so tight that they couldn't remove it. The baby needed to be out as soon as possible. The doctor raised his voice and told my friend to push hard. My friend was unaware of the gravity of the situation and asked if the baby was okay. I immediately encouraged her to push as hard as she could. She pushed harder without knowing the urgency of the moment—every second counted. The baby's shoulders passed through, and then the rest of her body:

it was a little girl! The doctors hurried to unwrap the umbilical cord from her neck, but the baby didn't cry or move. It was too late. They placed the baby on a cold medical table and rushed back to work on my friend as her life was in jeopardy!

I stood beside my lifeless godchild lying on the stainless-steel table—her body hadn't even been cleaned off. I didn't dare touch her as it was clear she wasn't breathing. Her tummy didn't move, and her face was blue! At first, I was shocked because the medical staff hadn't done more to save her. Then I realized that they felt they couldn't do anything for the infant and needed to attend to the mother's emergencies as a priority. They didn't tell the mother about her baby because they didn't want to alarm her and were focused on saving my friend's life. I consoled myself by thinking that at least my friend knew I was beside her baby. I felt helpless, filled with sadness and despair. I knew my friend had suffered more than enough in her abusive marriage and already had a lot to cope with as a newly single parent without having to bear the grief and devastation of losing her newborn. Then, I decided that this wouldn't be the outcome. This baby needed to live! I would not abandon this baby when she needed me the most. I was her godmother, after all! I was the last one who could make a difference. I had to do anything within my power that I could think of. I had to change the outcome. Could I do anything at this point?

My godchild was stillborn, lifeless. At that point in my life, I hadn't taken any healing courses, much less a prenatal one, but I had to do everything I possibly could. This was the moment when I needed to step up fully and access my inner healing power!

I put my two feet firmly on the hospital floor, grounding myself like never before. I asked the angels and archangels to be with me and to help me help the infant in front of me. I then put my hands above my godchild's body without touching her and decided that the purest white light would come through me to help her. I did not doubt it at all! I knew I was the last resort, but I also knew I wasn't alone, as I had my guides, angels, archangels, and deceased loved ones supporting me and sharing their power with me. I had faith that it would work. At this exact moment, my hands began to burn with energy, trembling as an enormous amount of white light passed through my hands into my godchild. This is when I heard her crying for the first time!

The doctor and nurses turned around, stunned and surprised to hear a baby's cry. One nurse immediately came over, took the baby, and put her upside down to clear her lungs, then cleaned her and put her in a blanket. My friend laughed as she said that her baby cried when she saw my face! Thankfully, the doctor was able to stabilize my friend, and she was unaware of what happened in those short moments with her infant. I said nothing about her baby's near-death experience so that she would stay calm and get some deep rest. I knew I had saved my godchild's life and was grateful for the miracle facilitated by the angels and unseen forces!

The bond between myself and my godchild is un-breakable, as she is like a daughter to me. We love each other with the deepest part of our hearts! Thank you, universe, as she is alive and well!

I am so proud of her and all her accomplishments. Her name is Emmanuelle, which means "God is with us." How perfect! I love you Emmanuelle! You will always be in my heart and my life! Thank you for always bringing me joy, laughter, light, and love. You are a miracle!

Bio

Sylvie Robert is a Shaman, an Amazing Healer, an International Spiritual Teacher, a Singing Medium and a Spirited Speaker. Sylvie is a Master Reiki and IET Master Instructor. She is a Chopra Center Certi-fied Instructor to teach Primordial Sound Meditation with Deepak Chopra, an Akashic Record Consultant, and a certified teacher with The Four Winds Society for Dying Consciously.

Sylvie has completed Shamanic Energy Medicine and Munay-ki with Alberto Villoldo. Sylvie is a Certified Angel Card Reader and Angel Numerologist with Radleigh Valentine. Sylvie completed The Journey Practitioner with Brandon Bays and studied advanced mediumship with Tim Abbot, John Holland, Sharon Anne Klingler, Janet Nohavec and Lisa Williams. Sylvie furthered her skills with the Shamans in Peru and studied with Neale Donald Walsch and Sonia Choquette. She is a Clutter and Clearing Coach with Denise Linn.

Sylvie has been seen for years on Rogers TV on Nat en Parle! www.facebook.com/munaysonko

Chapter 30

Plant Seeds in Fertile Soil

By Bonnie Rosensteel

T oxic seeds yield toxic fruits. Try and try as one might, a healthy harvest requires healthy roots, and sound earth to support their growing. For years, I attempted to grow myself and my life into a dream. The American dream. But I kept hitting dead end after dead end. I had lost connection with my intuition, unknowingly. Without it, I was like a ship lost at sea.

Self-knowledge is a key to consciousness ascension. In order to rise, I had to dig out what was buried. I was an archaeological dig site, and my skeletons were dinosaurs.

It is said that to understand the present, we must look to the past, which was something I'd been running from for years. The first step in resolving a problem is admitting there is one in the first place.

The artifacts of my past were things I preferred to keep underground until I could no longer. By the age of four, my little body had come to know the hands and dark thoughts of adult men, my innocence squandered. I was twelve when my mother abandoned us, and my father's strategic response was to avoid the issue, bare down, and work. At twenty years old, I enlisted in the US Army National Guard and served for seventeen years, where I perfected the art of emotion suppression, my brain broken down, and my individuality erased.

By the time I moved to Houston, Texas, in 2005 to attend grad school, majoring in music and vocal performance, I had become a shell of myself. My choice of Texas was one part love of warm weather, one part the quality of the school, and one part creating as much distance between mc and my past as possible. But everywhere I went, there I was, and until the victims of my subconscious were brought to light and allowed to heal, my life would continue to reflect what was hiding below. Wandering and lost, two thousand miles away from anyone I knew, I attracted yet more predators into my life.

Feelings signal our sensory experience of the world. Repressed emotions calcify those feelings, sinking the soul in the depths of Poseidon's grave. A body that feels disposable has had the experience of being disposed of. A body that has been used and battered retains and internalizes the violence inflicted. The nervous system adapts, mirroring the environment. Unresolved, the mind and body wage war against each other, fighting for sanity in this reality. In my case, the pain became too great, and my brain created a barrier between the two so that my bodily vessel could go on, if only as a ghost in this realm.

For years, I had learned how to play this part. My family of origin had groomed me to deny my emotions and intuition. My education taught me staged character performance. The army programmed the soldier mindset, persevering against all odds.

I perfected the art of appearing as if all was well on the surface, yet on the inside, I felt no joy. I never stopped moving forward, even while camouflaging insides that were rotting and falling apart. The dissonance became catastrophic when I had a mental health crisis in September of 2021. It was the darkest period of my life. I had resisted my past, and now I was in a hole. The question became, could I find my way out?

During my recovery, I came to discover that I had been disconnected from most of the physical sensations in my body. Somewhere between sexual assault and living with a violent abuser, my body went numb. From the neck down, I could hardly feel a thing, including my intuition. Both emotions and physical sensations had been muted and buried deep into my guts, organs, and muscle tissue. My body experienced daily sensations in muffled form, akin to hearing a radio playing while submerged under water. I was also seventy pounds overweight despite going to the gym six days a week, hiring a personal trainer, and maintaining a food diary and calorie counter.

The land of my body, my subconscious, was a toxic wasteland, incapable of growing life or manifesting any kind of dream worthy of the big screen. That which I did manifest was contradictory—my mind would ask for one thing, but the vibration of my disconnected body was attracting another. I attracted toxic relationships, narcissists, and purposeless work without understanding why. The road to Oz would be long, but now I was on it, and I had to put one foot in front of the other. Going back wasn't an option. The body is the subconscious. It houses memory. A complete excavation was required.

I had learned enough about healing at that point that I knew I should write the words I wished to experience. I wrote the words "I am safe," but my body shook violently.

I thought going to the gym was a form of self-care, and although I went every day, I was still overweight. My brain produced words that sounded nice, but the heart beating in my chest rejected these words and dreams, creating a contradictory loop of experience. My body didn't need more activity. It needed rest and gentleness. How could I attract or become what my body didn't believe or accept?

The turning point came in February of 2023. I attended a women's healing retreat hosted by a local facilitator I knew. Little did I know that a critical key would be introduced during this retreat that would break me open: at this retreat, we were taught to acknowledge, face, and feel our anger. Talk therapy and writing nice words were seeds, but the soil had to be cleansed. It was here I was given permission, for the first time in my life, to get angry, like a volcanic eruption dislodging and unearthing years of suppressed emotions in the depths of my guts.

I waged war on my past. I screamed and allowed hot tears to flow. I had a lot of work to do. Shortly after the retreat, I found myself at a smash therapy establishment where a hardwood nightstand fell victim to my arms wielding a sledgehammer. With this release of anger, my body responded. I began feeling physical sensations again, and at first, it was painful. Over twenty years of repressed energetic anger, previously calcified, was being released, and it hurt. Eventually, I began sleeping better, and the excess armor of weight I'd been carrying began melting off of me with very little effort. Once my internal world let go of the petrified feelings, so did my body let go of the need to carry the baggage.

Women are taught to be sweet and nice, sugar and spice. Anger is a "masculine" energy, and if, as a woman, I get mad, I become unlovable, illogical, and problematic. And yet, the number of things with which to be mad was long. Anger, vibrationally, is also an archaic emotion that evolved to signal to our evolutionary ancestors that a boundary had been violated. It was the emotion that energized us into action and initiated a fight or flight response. Anger activation was necessary to promote survival. I'd spent so much of my life putting my fuse out only to bury my anger into my gut, weighing my body and soul down, depleting me of my soul's energy.

The neurons that fire together wire together, and where attention goes, energy flows. First, I had to feel, and then I had to let go. Only then did the life I desired begin to manifest. Instead of toxic relationships, I began to attract genuine and balanced people. Opportunities began revealing themselves at work. Relationships I had long wanted to heal began to blossom. The universe doesn't send us what we want. She sends us what we are, and until we truly know what and who we are, including and especially what we harbor in our subconscious mind, we will continue to receive things we may not like. Awareness is the mother of perspective, and self-knowledge is the first step in manifesting what one truly desires. I am so grateful for the opportunity to continue to meet myself, every day. I am still learning, but now know the direction in which I am headed: one of my choosing. As above, so below.

Bio

Bonnie Rosensteel currently lives in Houston, Texas, with her husband and three dogs. She is an emotional intelligence and energy coach, community volunteer, US Army National Guard veteran, musician and poet. Bonnie believes that we are all capable of reaching our potential and magnifying our internal light, if only we know the way to find it.

Chapter 31

A Sky Full of Stars

By Bonnie Salkow

I knew I was in deep trouble when a good friend asked me what I wanted to accomplish more than anything in this world. I was ashamed to tell him that it was to weigh 128 pounds. After what felt like more than a lifetime of brutally wrestling with the demons of my addictions, at the age of 51, I was blessed with the gift of sobriety. After working the 12 steps, helping others, and trying countless antidepressants and every therapy imaginable, from EMDR to Electroshock Therapy, my mood swings were still debilitating. That feeling of, "Is this ever going to get better?" kept clawing at me. I was sober for over twelve years and found myself suicidal—again.

Hopelessly staring at the railroad tracks at 3 a.m ., I robotically drove straight into the parking lot of 7-Eleven, where I was temporarily distracted by rows of binge foods begging me to sweep them off the shelves. I became mesmerized by the pre-dawn dance of the Twinkies, twirling and singing, "Take me, take me!" Only a few steps away, Ben and Jerry's little cows stood glaring at me from their icy freezer, begging me to escort them to the warm safety of my home. "You, too, can be a fat cow. Eat me. And if I'm not enough, there's another pint, another flavor for you to grab." Those smug cows. Only a mere 1230 calories per pint. You know that no one eats just one pint. I lowered my eyes and shamefully paid for 2 pints of ice cream and the rest of the self-indulgent junk food in my cart.

I never believed I would be able to stop drinking, yet I had. The food binges, however, seemed insurmountable. I endlessly shoveled colossal amounts of food into my mouth, doubling over in excruciating pain, passing out, waking up, and starting all over. A blur of days often turned into weeks. I bared it all in my memoir, *Luv, Bonnie*. Yet even after my story was written, I still grappled with shame and confusion because my eating disorder, bipolar mood swings, borderline personality disorder, and my underlying trauma continued to bleed into every aspect of my life, destroying my self-esteem and countless relationships.

Several friends and professionals who had watched me stumbling over the years suggested I try Keta-

mine infusion therapy, including one friend in recovery who'd had astonishing results. Simply put,
this groundbreaking treatment in mental health and
treatment-resistant mental illnesses uses racemic
ketamine, an FDA-approved anesthesia, to target re-
ceptors and neurotransmitters in the brain, enhanc-
ing neuroplasticity and activating and creating new
pathways for permanent healing.

It took every ounce of determination I could muster
to drag myself off the floor and grasp for help. With
my recovery from alcohol and drugs a looming concern over my head, I initially scoffed at the Ketamine concept. But with my psychiatrist on board, I
became willing. An experienced and loving team of
board-certified and licensed professionals at the Ketamine & Wellness Clinic of South Florida created a
personalized therapeutic treatment plan for me consisting of six 45-minute infusions over 4 weeks combined with integral integration coaching sessions immediately before, after, and in between infusions for
support and guidance.

Sonia, my primary coach and earth Angel of mine for
sure, asked me one day before an infusion, "What are
you thinking right before you binge?" I always knew
that I was either avoiding my feelings or punishing
myself. Either way, I was hurting myself. Then came
her million-dollar question. "Why do you want to

hurt yourself?" The reason was quite simple. I *hated myself.* And there it was. The root of everything.

"So-and-so doesn't love me. I'm not as pretty, young, or talented as so-and-so. My face is wrinkled. I'm fat. I'm old." I didn't focus on how many people loved me because there were tons of them. I was worried about the ones that didn't. I didn't focus on how many people told me I'd helped them on their journey in life. Because I couldn't change my life. I couldn't stop binging. I couldn't lose weight. Then, in a flash, it hit me. For the first time in my life. I don't *have* to lose weight! That voice of needing to be thin was my mother's voice that I'd taken on long ago. She'd been gone over 10 years, yet little Bonnie, that little girl inside of me, had grabbed the knife from her and continued stabbing it right into my heart. That enlightening moment happened during the integration process right after my infusion.

Epiphanies washed over me like falling stars across the brilliant night sky. I see the good in me, the bad in me, the entire picture of who I am. It dawned on me that I am much more than my looks. That incessant voice that had pounded in my head every single day of my life, "I can't, I can't, I can't," has disappeared. I realized I could do anything. I'm a survivor. All the hardships I've overcome became crystal clear. It's so much easier to love myself than it was not to. For years, I tried everything to achieve perfection. I'm not Barbie. I'm Bonnie. That's so much better because I'm real, and she isn't. I thought it was about what I did, who I was with, how I looked, what I drove, what if they didn't like me? It was all so exhausting. Those berating voices in my head never shut up. Suddenly, I don't care. It doesn't even matter. Because I like myself.

Magically awakened, I don't want to hurt myself anymore. So, I seek ways to feel good and make the right choices to do that. I'll feel fat if I eat 2 gallons of ice cream and 6 Twinkies. So I make other food choices.

That "no one cares" voice I used to hear is a lie. I want friends, so I no longer push those I care about away. It doesn't matter what other people think of me anymore. Nothing is that big of a deal. I'm confident that I'm loved, safe, strong, and capable. I'm free.

Integration included several transformational exercises. I made a happy list of all the things little Bonnie loved doing. I wrote down what my ideal day would be. I do these things today.

I made an ongoing list of my negative thoughts and countered them with positive thoughts. Those negative thoughts are debilitating lies I tell myself or thoughts that will only drag me down. For example, "Why bother to do anything? I'm going to sit here alone." Countered with, "My purpose is to get out and spread the knowledge that I've been through hell, and I've come out the other side."

I made a list of who the *real* Bonnie is. I'm no longer just a face or a body in the mirror. I'm a good friend. I'm creative. I'm passionate about many things. I show up for my friends. I love fresh air and the wind. I am these things and more. Not what I look like.

I wake up in the morning and, fully undressed, look into my eyes in the mirror, say "I love you, Bonnie" 20 times, and then write down 2 things I like about myself. At first, I nearly choked as I uttered the words. It gets much easier as time goes on.

I never believed loving myself was a possibility in this lifetime. Accepting myself is loving myself. And I've achieved that. The chatter whispers in my ear every so often but quickly dissipates as I march on, whole and perfect exactly the way I am.

Bio

From the moment she was born in the suburbs of New York City, Bonnie's only purpose was to marry a rich guy, look pretty, and lose weight. That was quite a difficult burden to carry. As a result, she turned to food, drugs, alcohol, and unhealthy relationships to fill the emptiness inside her.

She ended up in a multitude of treatment centers, psych hospitals, bars, and convenience stores, drowning in her own misery. At 51, she was finally graced with the gift of sobriety from the angels that had been with her all along. Thus began her beautiful and profound spiritual journey. Her true and captivating story was brought to life when *Luv, Bonnie*, her first book, was published in 2022.

Shining her light on many others suffering from addiction in various 12-step programs is vital to her spiritual growth.

Bonnie has always been enchanted by the thrill of Broadway musicals, performing, singing, and dancing. Her other passions include creating whimsical art objects, nature, travel, exploring what lies beyond the fourth dimension, and her dogs. Today, Bonnie lives in Miami with her cherished Teacup Yorkie and is filled with love, gratitude, peace, and joy. She can be reached at cocomundy@yahoo.com.

Chapter 32

I Dare You To TRI

By Felicia Shaviri

"Be brave enough to take the necessary steps to create the life you envision."
—Felicia Shaviri

At one time or another in our lives, we have been challenged by a friend, relative, or someone in our circle or even ourselves to a dare. Some accepted the challenges in the dares to break the rules, say hello to someone they liked, take something that didn't belong to them, or even pick a fight with another for no other reason than to test the individual.

The "dare" is a complex yet inherent fascination of humans pushing the boundaries by testing the limits of possibility. A dare often carries negative consequences, such as the potential for harm or injury, and quickly puts us on alert when we hear the word dare.

It's important to remember that some dares, when accepted with thoughtful responsibility, contribute to the individual and others in the areas of personal growth mentality, physically and spiritually leading us on a path of a life we may not have otherwise known. I truly believe this combination of life-building propels us in a direction to conquer our fears, boost our self-confidence and self-esteem, and develop problem-solving skills and new skill sets we can use throughout our lives.

After being introduced to the sport of running by a coworker and participating in a fun run, I was hooked. I was lacing up my sneakers and hitting the pavement every chance I got. There was nothing comparable to how running made me feel. It not only impacted my day but my life. I felt alive and present in the world with each step. When the endorphins kicked in, it allowed me to experience euphoria like I had never known.

I decided to subscribe to Northwest Runner, a running magazine in the Pacific Northwest with a list of upcoming runs, tips for gear, and inspirational stories from other runners. If my memory serves me correctly, the magazine subscription was 10 bucks, and I was making $7.45 an hour, and it was worth it. I read the same magazine from cover to cover.

I can remember reading an article about an accountant whose friend invited her to do a 10k with her. The accountant informed her friend that she was not a runner. The friend encouraged her to give it a try and made it clear to her that it was just fine. The account was accepted and placed amongst the top finishers. She continued with her running and improved her time. Not long after, she was invited to try a triathlon, where you would swim, bike, and run, and yes, she did accept, and she placed as well. As I read the article, I was full of inspiration for the seed that had been planted.

Several years passed, and many life-changing events took place. I was now married, and we received the most precious gift of a beautiful baby girl. I continued running and even invested in a jogging stroller to take her along with me. I didn't have much time for anything else other than a quick run, caring for my family and work. Then, one day, I saw an advertisement in one of the athletic magazines for "The Danskin Women's Triathlon Race Series." I scanned the advertisement for the cities that would be hosting these events, and Seattle was one of them!

The distance for the event was a 0.5 mile swim, 12.4 mile bike with a 3.1 mile run to complete the course. Although I felt pretty confident with the running and bike legs, I did not feel confident with the swim.

Yes, I could swim, although I was never taught how. I essentially learned how to swim by watching my siblings swim in the local pools. The difference here was it was open water, Lake Washington. I read any and everything I could get my hands on regarding triathlons and how to prepare and train.

Using a spiral notebook, I created a planner for training days. I would run in the a.m. with my daughter in the jogger, and on the days that I would bike, she rode in the child carrier attached to my seat. I had a membership at the YMCA, where I swam.

It was finally race day. I picked up my race packet the day before and laid everything out on the bureau before bed. The anticipation was almost too much. I was excited, but yet there was this underlying fear that I may not come back. There was a thought of Jaws, the Loch Ness monster, or even the creature from the Black Lagoon, sweeping me under, never to be heard of again.

Before leaving, I wrote a note to my family, sharing with them how much I loved them and how much they meant to me. Although I was afraid of swimming in the open water, I also knew it was important that I face my fear. I drove to Seattle, found a park with ease, detached my bike, grabbed my gym bag, and walked over to the bike transition area to set up my gear. The entire time, I could hear her voice in my head, telling me, "Felicia, you're not gonna die. I know you're scared, but you can do this."

Standing at the edge of the water, waiting for my age group to begin the swim. I was filled with sheer panic. There was a voice in my head now telling me, "You don't have to do this." "If you are that afraid, you can walk away. No one is forcing you to do this." So, I agreed with that voice, "You're right, I don't have to do this." Overwhelmed by fear, I turned around to leave, and there was a sea of women full of excitement, eager to participate in this event. It was magical. What stood out the most for me on that day was the woman I saw with a prosthetic leg, who inspired me to turn back towards the water with newfound determination to do the dang thing.

Off went the air horn, and in went my group, taking the position of far back and right (slower swimmers...me), flinging my body into the water without thinking, I reminded myself that I was not going to die, the entire swim. Yes, I survived the swim and cried from one transition to the next, even when I crossed the finish line. This event was a dare that I placed on myself because I wanted to know if it was possible. At the core of a foundation I was and continue to build upon. Every aspect of my life was affected because I dared myself to do something that I had never done before. It was a boost in confidence, self-esteem, physical fitness, mental strength, and overall personal achievement.

Dear Reader: What do you desire, past, present, or future? What would you want to have come to fruition in your life? What holds you back consciously or subconsciously from making your desire a reality? If your desire came true, how do you think it would affect your life?

Remember This

You are capable of achieving your dreams and desires.

You have the power to release any limitations.

Your superpower is believing in yourself.

You are a pretty amazing human.

Bio

Felicia Shaviri, a native of Chicago's Englewood District, is on a mission to tell everyone within earshot or afar the importance of the role they play in the world. A former Corrections Deputy turned author and Wellness Coach, Felicia believes every person can turn their life around regardless of the circumstances. "I stand fast with an unbending belief that there is always an opportunity to learn and grow with every experience. Each experience offers us endless possibilities to live the life we desire." Felicia is a Professional Fitness/Wellness Coach, Certified Life Coach, Reiki Practitioner, Voice Over Talent, and Founder of SheRox Fitness and Wellness.

For questions, comments or interest in trying a TRI, contact her at feliciashaviri.com or follow her on @feliciashaviri on Instagram.

Chapter 33

Brighten the Mundane With Magical Miracles

By YuSon Shin

Between life's milestones and setbacks, there are long stretches that feel monotonous. We trade our childhood patterns of "home to school, school to home" for the adult ritual of "home to work, work to home." While on the hamster wheel of life, we are deceived into thinking that the harder we try, the faster and further we will go. During these periods, exhaustion sets in, our eyes roll back into our heads and our senses dull from boredom and stagnation. What used to be in brilliant color feels like a dim world in dull shades of gray. This is when we need an injection of magic and miracles to infuse color back into our lives, much like the scene in *The Wizard of*

Oz when the tornado transports Dorothy into the brilliantly colorful and magical land of Oz.

Reality feels mundane, requiring blood, sweat, and tears to push us forward. Magic, however, is unexpected, effortless, and feels created by a power greater than our efforts. Magic leaves us wide-eyed and wanting more, eliciting joy, wonder, astonishment, mystery, and feelings that anything is possible. It makes us believe that we can fly and create something from nothing. Magic and miracles provide the stepping stones through the boring parts of life, acting as magical breadcrumbs and inspiration through hard times. These are the times when it feels like God stops by for a visit.

There are different forms of magic. Theurgy, known as divine or supernatural magic, is the collaboration between human beings and God. Thaumaturgy, on the other hand, is practical magic, the capability of an individual like a magician to work magic or a saint to perform miracles. Perhaps we are more inclined to believe in theurgy because we think only miracles can be created by a mighty force outside of ourselves. Whatever form of magic shows up, if it's not a miracle on par with parting the Dead Sea, we tend to chalk it up to luck or a random event. When miracles do occur, it helps to acknowledge them and be thankful. Experiencing miracles makes us feel special and chosen, and they have the power to change us.

I wish I had known at an earlier age that the ability to create magic and miracles can be learned. Unfortunately, I did not learn from my parents. They would be best described as dream killers. It wasn't until I was in my 40s that I felt I had some distance from my upbringing, a level of financial security, and a stronger sense of self to ditch old programming from my parents. When I stopped caring about what other people thought, I could finally play. Playing pulled magic more consistently into my life, bringing color back into my world.

I played the "Wouldn't It Be Nice" game. I found that this game was beyond the reach of self-sabotage. Concerns about worthiness, deservingness, or taking from others if I accepted abundance didn't affect this game. I was simply asking, "Wouldn't it be nice if...?" When I filled in the blanks with all I could ever wish for, the answer was always "Yes. Yes, it would be nice." There was never a "but" because the question doesn't entertain any "buts." So, I let myself wish for more and it felt good to envision having all the nice things with all my senses. The more magic showed up, the more I expected. The frequency of magic and miracles increased like the upward swirl of a magic wand.

Imagine being in a magical house where all you have to do is to raise your hand and think about what you want in the house and the object levitates off the shelf and flies right into your hand. This is manifestation magic. Real-life magic can look different but still have the same result. I wanted to swim with wild dolphins in Hawaii, but work and finances were formidable barriers. Then, work deadlines shifted, and I received a bonus.

Imagine being able to turn lead into gold. This is using alchemy and manifestation magic. Have you ever received an unexpected check or found money on the floor? I had a rental house with an HVAC unit that died in August. The replacement cost was $6,000, which I didn't have. I was sweating from anxiety and crying crocodile tears before I pulled myself together. In a day, the money showed up. This miracle helped me deal with a crazy tenant.

Imagine receiving a visitation from an angel, butterfly, dragonfly, or hummingbird. Once, I went for a walk with my dog Peanut and I saw a butterfly in someone's garden. I felt the urge to hold out my finger, and immediately, the butterfly landed and stayed for a while. It felt like my Snow White magical moment. I know I've been visited countless times by earth angels that help at just that right moment, and I never see them again. I hope to be an angel to someone to pay it forward.

Imagine putting your hands on someone who is hurting or dying, and the healing magic saves a life. I have worked on many humans and animals with cancer and other physical issues and had them heal completely. One of my clients had a grapefruit-sized cancerous mass in the colon and, with consistent healing, is now healthy. Medical miracles are real.

Imagine having unexplained events happen. One day at dusk, while walking with Peanut, we stopped at the stair landing because three green-blue lights at varying heights seemed to slowly meander and rise from below the stairwell toward the blue-violet ombré night sky. We both just watched until they disappeared. I live in Los Angeles where we do not have fireflies. Nothing could explain what we saw. There have been a handful of times when bright white lights were floating around in my bedroom at night. I have blackout blinds, so it couldn't have been a reflection of any light source. This is another magical mystery. Years ago, I had to drive a five-hour detour to Santa Barbara for a weekend workshop because of a landslide on the main freeway. I got up super early to get there for the morning start. I didn't realize how drowsy I was. I fell asleep at a curve in the road and

I awoke as I was driving out of the curve. That was a life-saving miracle.

It sounds crazy, but I have learned to collaborate with God on mini-miracles. My mom recently fell and fractured her pelvis in four places and landed in the emergency room and eventually a skilled nursing center. The week of the accident, I noticed that I had half the usual client load for the week. In the chaos and concern that ensued after I was notified of my mom's fall, I knew that it was by design. In co-creating with God, my calendar frees up and fills up as needed. Someone else might not notice, but I know that magic continues to guide and help me.

Sometimes, when there is a decision to be made between two paths to take, I ask for a sign that is meaningful to me. If this path is the one to take, please show me a hummingbird doing the mating dance of flying up and down in a J formation until it does the grand finale of flying straight up to heaven to finish with a near-vertical dive and a high-pitched "Whee!" The miracle in this sign lies in getting this sign even when the mating season has long ended.

Don't wait for life or magic to happen. We often credit the big magician in the sky, but his magic lives in all of us. There is a powerful magician within each of us. Create the life you want. As Glinda the Good Witch from *The Wizard of Oz* reminded us, "You've always had the power, my dear; you just had to learn it for yourself."

Bio

YuSon Shin is a gifted healer, intuitive, medium, speaker, author, and teacher of the healing and intuitive arts based in Los Angeles. With her trademark joyful and compassionate demeanor, she uses her gifts to help people and pets heal from physical, emotional, and spiritual ailments. YuSon loves teaching and holds workshops designed to help students awaken their spiritual superpowers. She believes everyone has the power to heal themselves.

YuSon is an expert practitioner in a wide variety of healing techniques because she feels there is no "one size fits all" when working with her clients. She utilizes Akashic records and Chinese energy healing techniques to perform past life, karma and ancestral clearings. She is also a practitioner of the Bengston Energy Healing Method. She is a certified Reiki Master and also uses Integrated Energy Therapy, 5th Dimensional Quantum Healing, Quantum Touch, DNA Theta, and Access Bars. She is the author of eight books.

She can be reached at YuSon@ShinHealingArts.com and www.ShinHealingArts.com.

Chapter 34

Crazy Socks with Crocs and Other 50's Magic

By Jeannie Soverns

My 50s are the magical invisible decade. I remember when my friend Barbara told me the same thing when she was in her 50s. It can be tough to feel invisible, especially when you're used to being noticed. I want you to know that you're not alone. It's a time when we're often seen as being too old to be young and too young to be old. We're still determining where we fit in. But that doesn't mean we're not valuable. We have a lot to offer the world, even if we don't always feel like it. I remember when I was young, I was always on fire. I was the youngest, brightest, and funniest in the group, the office, the party, or wherever. I was always noticed. Then I got older, and my neck looked like a turkey. People start-ed calling me ma'am, and I felt invisible.

I kept on being me, and I'm going to keep on shin-ing bright. In the last year, I received my bache-lor's degree, after starting college 31 years ago. I also received my ministerial degree, co-founded a New Thought Church community, and purchased my first home with my partner of almost 10 years. This is me in my invisible decade, rocking it! I am the co-founder of Begin Within Ministries. This is where I manifested the magic of this decade. Our first service was about *being authentically ourselves*. My co-founder and friend Michelle Davis, RScP, and I knew we would run into situations where we would be raw and real and that those who like light and polite may have issues with us. It was, and is, impor-tant to us that people know who we are and what we are about. In this world today, I realize how impor-tant being clear, being kind, and being authentic is. Authenticity is not only desired but necessary. Too many people are drowning in themselves, afraid to reach out for help, for community, for a life they love living. Some have been stuck since the pandemic began, and they need a place where they feel seen, heard, and safe to be authentically themselves. Some people have been stuck there their whole lives.

It tugged on my mind that people may not like us. I had to spend time with myself in prayer, getting honest if I could handle people not wanting to be part of our ministry. Those worries were unfounded. We have a core group of people who attend regularly in person, on Facebook, YouTube, and Instagram. One partner got up in the middle of the night to watch us when she traveled to Australia for vacation.

Michelle and I sit on our sofa each week and chat with our audience. We give out affirmation cards with our topic. Our goal is to have an inspirational deck of cards by the end of the year. I love the idea of a club versus a building or church. We want to be a place of communal gathering.As we continue to evolve, we hope to inspire others to evolve as well. Eventually, we hope to franchise the idea.

I laugh and say, "Have a slipcover and pillows, will travel." I know what we bring to the world is needed and wanted. Some days, it seems surreal that this is my life today. As a spiritual life coach, a 12-step sponsor, a friend, a mentor, a partner, a manager, and a minister, my code is to create a safe space for others to be authentic and vulnerable. This is the type of person I needed growing up, the one I searched for. When I had cancer, when I left my spiritual community after a decade, this is who I cried out for. This is who I believe is needed when I look in my mirror.

I think that many people have attempted to do this for me in my life, and some are better than others, and I am grateful for all of them. They are the reason I continue to reach out to be available for those who are in need.

There are times when I feel so fabulous and that everything flows in life, and then there are the times when my body is acting as if it doesn't know it's whole, perfect, and complete, and it hurts to breathe because I have part of my lung removed due to cancer. There are days that I roll out of bed because I cannot sit up straight. There are moments when I suck all the air out of the room because my knee gave out. There are freakout days and grief days. There are days when I'm not sure this is working out for me and that I'm not cut out for the career I'm in. I am becoming so aware of who I am as a person and my foibles.

I am a PQ Coach working on my certification, and I help introduce others to some of our internal saboteurs like the judge, the victim, the avoider, and the people pleaser, to name a few. These are characteristics that, growing up, kept me safe and secure and allowed me to negotiate through some tough days and dark nights of the soul, but I don't need them so much anymore.

People have called me a warrior and have told me how strong I am with all the things I've been through the last few years. I see where I have appreciated that recognition and have found myself playing it to my favor for sure. It takes tenacity to continue to learn and grow. I have a friend, Susan, who turned 80 and recently lost her partner of 50 years. She is in classes and is growing and doing and moving her body, mind, and spirit. She is a warrior.

I wear compression socks with my Crocs. I wear bright, beautiful caftans. I wear gaudy jewelry and unique glasses. I figured I might as well enjoy this so-called invisible decade. It is filled with beautiful curves of dark and light clouds. I have traveled through forests and green growing edges. I've been lost in deserts with no rainwater. In my fabulous magical 50s, I have gained and lost friends. I have mourned opportunities I thought I frivolously wasted. I have celebrated days that I never thought I would see. I have been thin and hungry, fat and happy, and everything in between.

The thrill of finding myself after 50 years is like a second childhood. I finally got to be the person I was meant to be. I have let go of all the expectations and obligations that society has placed on me and be myself. I can explore my passions and interests without judgment. I can make new friends, make new mistakes and try new things. I can live my life to the fullest, and I do.

It's not always easy, of course. There are times when I feel lost or confused. But it's all worth it because I realize that I am stronger and more resilient than I ever thought possible.

So, if you're over 50 and you're feeling lost, don't worry. You're not alone. And it's not too late to find yourself. Take some time to explore your inner world and figure out what makes you happy. And then go put on your crazy socks and Crocs!

Bio

Religious Science Minister Rev. Jeannie Soverns embraces love, humor, and authenticity by engaging in the adventure of life. She has dipped her toes in many arenas, such as spiritual life coaching, stand-up comedy, local theater, cake artistry, travel, writing, and even skydiving. With over 26 years of 12-step recovery that aligns with her spiritual growth journey, Rev. Jeannie offers those who are in recovery a sacred space by harmoniously embracing the principles of the 12 steps and Science of Mind philosophy. She believes in her mission to be a safe container for hugs, comfort, humor, and compassion to those ready to live their best life. She is the co-founder of Begin

Within Ministries, which exists to inspire others toward a deeper connection with spirit while creating a life they love. The Sunday service is called *Sofa Sundays*, and this is not your mama's church. This is a dynamic, fun, and interactive service, encouraging conversations, questions and seeking the mystery of the divine, unfiltered, vulnerable, and real.

Contact Jeannie at BeginWithinMinistries.com or Sofasundaysjs@gmail.com

Chapter 35

A Line in the Sand

By Alicia Sweezer

We all have a point in our lives where we say it is now or never. One of these moments occurred in my life when I was searching for a new place to live. The house I was living in was being sold, so I had 30 days to find a new home. My finances were limited at the time; therefore, I was not in a situation where I could arbitrarily pick anywhere I wanted to live. You can imagine the level of fear that comes with something like this, as well as all the *what ifs*. I was currently living alone, which I loved, and living alone is ideal because I have my business and see clients, etc. In addition, I had some severe trauma from living with narcissistic sociopathic roommates and I did not want to go back to a roommate situation.

This reality says that with limited financial resources, you cannot be choosy, you cannot have desires, and you absolutely cannot have what you want. You must take what is available and be happy with that. I decided at that moment I was going to trust and listen to my intuition 100%. In all the other areas of my life, I do this naturally. When we are afraid of things like not having enough money, shelter, etc., it is easy to fall into the old patterns of doing, figuring it out, and worrying instead of staying in a place of being. We go out mindlessly searching from a place of fear and limitation instead of pulling the things we desire to us.

In this situation, I decided to take one of my biggest fears in life and create what I wanted. I wrote my ideal home list, drew a conscious line in the sand, and committed to it no matter what. I was only going to do what I was intuitively guided to do to help me find a new home. I would not look for a place unless I was guided to it. I wouldn't talk about it with people unless I was guided to. Now, did this have its moments of what in the world am I doing? Yes! And it is okay; we get to love the human part of us. We get to acknowledge the fear and all the other feelings and tell ourselves it is okay.

To my surprise, the people around me struggled with the way I was finding a new home. They cared about me and along with that came their limiting beliefs, fears, and wanting to fix. So, in addition to my inner struggle, I was now combating theirs. Often, our spiritual classrooms include additional challenges like this—yaaa!

For the first week, I received no intuitive messages; it was quiet. This is where you can start to question yourself (on many levels), and self-doubt can take hold if you allow it. I dug in and embraced what I'd committed to. Then, I got the intuitive hit to ask a friend (Michelle) about a possible housing opportunity. She was a facilitator of a house that might be up for rent. Without checking with the homeowners, Michelle said, "No, it wasn't an option to rent to me." I blindly accepted this answer. This was a critical point for me later.

Next, I received a message to look online for another possibility. There was an amazing guest house that could potentially be perfect for me. I started the process of discovery, and it turned out to be a scam. Luckily, my intuition guided me about the scam before I had any financial consequences. I was devastated, scared, and confused, and I wanted to give up my commitment to find a new home intuitively. My intuition led me to this guest house. How could it not be the one for me? I allowed the self-doubt questions to come in. What did I miss? What did I do wrong?

What if my intuition is not working correctly? Then, I crushed those thoughts and reinforced my commitment to myself. I now had one week to find a new home.

As a backup plan, my friend Michelle offered me a bedroom in her house. My cat Pip would need to stay in the room 24/7, and I would once again have roommates. This option also brought additional challenges because I run my business from home and see clients. It would be hard to do all of that in one bedroom. I was grateful to have a backup plan even though it was not what I desired.

As I stood looking at this bedroom with now 3 days left to find a new place to live, I thought to myself, if I had to move in here, I would die. I am not being dramatic; it felt like death. It felt like moving backward, and everything in my body said no. At that moment, I mustered my strength and asked Michelle if I could talk directly to the homeowners to ask if I could rent their home. We called them, and they said yes. Within the next 36 hours, I moved into a house that I had all to myself with a rent that was a match for me. It was surreal. So many times, we think that doing something intuitively means it will be calm and relaxed the whole way. It can be, and a lot of times, it brings an amazing roller coaster of growth and healing opportunities that change my life forever.

This is an example of how you cannot miss what the universe has for you. If you are like me, that can mean occasionally, we take the long way. In the beginning, I could have said I wanted to talk to the homeowners myself instead of listening to what Michelle said, but I did not. I was not strong enough in that moment. I then manifested additional situations about one of my biggest fears (shelter) to strengthen my commitment to live an intuitively guided life. When you continually slay the biggest fear dragons in your life, the growth and healing you receive is immeasurable, and the trust you gain not only in the universe but in yourself is forever.

Bio

Why do people try to fit themselves in a box that was never meant for them? As a scientific psychic, Alicia Sweezer knows what it's like to not fit into any box! As a former wildlife biologist of endangered species, she uses her super analytical skills alongside her keen intuitive gifts to help her clients make tremendous foundational changes in their mindset, behaviors, and relationships. She uses these same skills for her animal clients, too, as an Animal Communicator. Alicia has been breaking through limiting beliefs her whole life. From being told that her career working with endangered species was virtually impossible to healing after multiple traumatic brain injuries when people told her she would have to live in a care facility, Alicia is a living miracle. Overcoming narcissistic and relationship abuse and healing deep trauma, Alicia has used the tools she shares with her clients to be happy and have amazing relationships while living her purpose. Alicia guides her clients to create the life they desire by connecting with the Truth of who they really are and helping them bring their unique gifts to the world. Alicia wants you to know anything is possible! Connect with Alicia at: www.whoknewhealing.com

Chapter 36

Superpowers are Real

By Jacque Tarlton

What it was like

L ittle did I realize the profound impact May 15, 2012, would have on my life. That is my sobriety date, and getting where I am now was not easy. So, let me back up, and I'll give you a little snippet of what my life was like—what it was *really* like, not my highlight reel and how it looked on the outside.

From the beginning, I was always a dreamer, from playing with my dolls to creating real-life fantasies with my friends and with my sister. On one of our family trips, my sister and I acted like we were twins visiting the US from another country. We were frolicking in the ocean and speaking gibberish with each other. We got attention alright, but we did not fool anyone.

I am the middle child. My younger brother was super chill. My sister and I would gang up on him, until one day he got big, and by big, I mean strong, enough to fight back. Looking back, I feel horrible for the torture I put him through, and I am truly grateful that he is a forgiving soul and we have a beautiful relationship today.

I looked up to my big sister because, in my eyes, she had everything: she was smart, beautiful, and popular. So, I was like a chameleon and would take on whatever energy she was putting out. But this went well beyond being around my sister. I did this in all areas of my life: around family, in school, with my friends, and in social situations. I never learned to tune into how I felt or how to express *my* feelings. I taught myself how to match my energy to the energies of the situation I was in.

But all of that changed at a party in the eighth grade.

I was trying out for the dance team at my middle school, so I had to learn a choreographed routine. I have always been self-conscious about the way I look, move, and act, which held me back from reaching my full potential in this performance. After try-outs, one of my friends had a party. There was alcohol at the party, and of course, I had a couple of drinks. I vividly remember feeling more secure and outgoing when I drank that alcohol. I was dancing uninhibitedly, and I was talking to people I would never have been able to start a conversation with. When my mom picked me up from the party, she even complimented me on how well I was dancing and how I had come out of my shell.

My alcohol addiction was sneaky. It started pretty—I was engaging and the life of the party. Without alcohol, I was a painfully shy little girl. My face would turn beet red if I had to talk in front of a group or if all the attention was on me. My birthdays were traumatic experiences—I hated everyone singing "Happy Birthday" to me because my face would turn so red. I was painfully self-conscious of it, which made it even worse, and my face would stay red longer.

Alcohol changed everything. When that magic elixir went into my body, I was able to be the young girl or young woman I wanted to be, and I was able to do anything.

The fairy tale of alcohol being my superpower did not last long.

What Happened

I wish I could say I learned that alcohol was my kryptonite when I was kicked off of the cheerleading squad my senior year in high school (cheerleading was my *life*), when I got a DUI in college, or when I was raped, or even when a boyfriend that I now lovingly refer to as the "dead doctor" overdosed for the up-teenth time and passed away.

All of those were giant alarms the universe was sending me that would normally stop people in their tracks and make them re-evaluate what they are doing in their lives. Not me. Instead, I turned to alcohol, usually in the form of one or two bottles of wine every night.

During the day, I appeared to be doing well: I had an amazing job, I was traveling the world for work and pleasure, and I married my best friend.

But on the inside, I was broken. I still had not learned how to feel my feelings, but I always got a reprieve at the end of the day with my lover and best friend: a bottle of wine.

I was miserable at my "dream job" because it did not align with me energetically. I was making bad decisions when I was drunk—thank goodness social media was not big back then! I drank until I passed out every night, so when I woke up, I had to deal with the wreckage I created. I felt like my husband was absent (but I came to realize it was *me* who was absent).

The bottom line is I felt horrible, and I was at my "spiritual bottom."

My one true love, alcohol, had stopped working for me. One drink was too much, and one thousand drinks was never enough.

What it's Like Now

On May 15, 2012, I embarked on the journey of my lifetime. I started to realize that the only thing that needed to change was *everything*. That may sound daunting, but it is quite refreshing. I *get* to dream again; I *get* to realize those dreams. I *get* to do hard things—and they are all hard things!

There is something immensely powerful in slowing down and becoming present. Key mindset changes in my transformation to an alcohol-free life were the shift from self-centeredness and isolation to one of service and connection. By helping others in their journey to a healthier lifestyle or in their journey to recovery, I not only stayed on track but also created beautiful experiences with them and for myself. Being part of a supportive community and making a difference in the lives of others has been spiritually rewarding.

I have manifested remarkable things in my life, both before recovery and since being alcohol-free. While drinking, I manifested dream jobs and incredible travel. In recovery, I have been able to manifest incredible opportunities, but most importantly, I am now manifesting beautiful *inward* experiences.

One of the most powerful tools for manifesting spiritual enlightenment is having a purpose in life. Knowing that purpose, you should then ask yourself, "What do you want to create?" Having a clear vision of what you want to create and using *all* your senses is a powerful manifesting tool.

I saved a picture of a woman wearing a beautiful red flowy dress, swinging over the rice fields in Bali. I would look at it occasionally, envisioning myself swinging over the rice field with a group of incredible women: I could *feel* the warm breeze on my skin as I was gliding above the rice fields, I could *see* the beautiful green rice patties, I could *taste* the mildly sweet and crisp lemongrass tea and *smell* the ginger and mint notes in the tea, and I could *hear* the Bali nature sounds as I would drift off to sleep.

I had tears of joy when I led a group of twelve women to Bali for a spiritual connection retreat. The connections we created will last a lifetime. The spiritual experience we all had was an uplifting, energetic and peaceful feeling that we will all carry in our memories forever.

Being an alcoholic was my biggest secret, and now I consider being an alcoholic in recovery my greatest superpower. If you have an addiction or a secret, there is nothing more powerful than turning your challenges into opportunities. This will help you uncover your true potential so you can manifest a life beyond your wildest dreams.

Bio

Jacque has always been a dreamer. She is passionate about living a healthy life. She loves sharing how fun it can be to be healthy, both mentally and physically. She is a coach, a student of life, and a retreat leader. She enjoys working out with friends, traveling the world with her husband, and spending time with friends and family. She lives in Miami with her husband, where they overlook the beautiful and calming waters of Biscayne Bay.

Acknowledgments

I would like to thank my husband, Charles, for sticking by my side, believing in me, and supporting all my crazy dreams. Thanks to my mom, Connie, and stepfather, Tom, who prayed for me continuously, to my brother and sister, Lance and Stephanie, and their supportive spouses for their love. And lastly, to all my friends who have been there for me through thick and thin, darkness and light: I love and appreciate you!

You can reach Jacque via Instagram @jacquetarlton

Chapter 37

Follow the Signs

By Chris Turpyn

My journey of awakening began in December 2010. At the time, I was forty-one years old and working for a company that managed Homeowners' Associations. My career had been in real estate, primarily working in affordable housing. I did not have a college degree, having only completed a few classes, but I had successfully worked my way up in the real estate management field and was living a comfortable life. I had a nice home and a loving relationship and believed I was living the proverbial dream. I then received a phone call that my daughter had been in what can only be described as a freak accident. My only child died two days later at the age of twenty.

Parents spend their lives trying to shield their children from each little bump and scrape. As a parent, I lived on a constant defensive, trying to avoid any potential harm to her. Wear your bicycle helmet, be careful crossing the street, call me when you get to your friend's house. All the safety boxes had been checked for twenty years, and then she was gone. I could not come to terms with the nature of her death. She lived in an upstairs apartment, and someone ran a gas generator inside the house while they were doing renovations. She was asleep, and the generator's carbon monoxide permeated up through the vents. She died of carbon monoxide poisoning. How was that possible? That was never on the list of potential hazards in my mind, so surely, I let my guard down, and this was all my fault. I found myself evaluating every decision I had ever made. I was angry at everyone and at time itself. I could not fathom how time continued when my world had stopped. I struggled to breathe. I did not know how I was going to survive. I was drowning in an ocean of what-if and if-only scenarios.

I have always had a strong relationship with God, although I do not attend church regularly. I begged God to take me instead of her during those two days at the hospital. Was my relationship with God not strong enough? Was I not a good person? What could I have done differently? After she died, I felt an intentional need to join her in case she was frightened because I now questioned my faith in the afterlife. My faith was shattered, and I needed help. Unbeknownst to me at the time, my partner had a conversation with my daughter at the hospital in which they talked about me should she not survive the accident. "Your mom is not going to be okay if she doesn't know that you are." Help was on the way.

The first sign came to me the day after she died. I was updating friends and extended family using social media, so I picked up my phone to check comments. On the top of my social media page appeared a white, glowing orb. I showed my partner and family, and no one had seen anything like that before. I took a screenshot of it. I was talking to my daughter regularly, the conversations consisting of apologies and regrets, begging her to let me know if she was okay. Could that be her? It was difficult to ignore, even for a skeptic who desperately wanted to blame herself for everything that had transpired.

The next day was spent having to plan for the funeral. It was the worst time of my life. At the house, there was a blur of visitors and a flurry of food drop-offs. My partner and brother went to my daughter's apartment to pick up her belongings. I couldn't bring myself to go. I was numb to things happening around me. I didn't want to eat, I didn't want to talk, and I didn't know how to keep going. That night, my partner plugged my daughter's cell phone in to charge it. My daughter woke up early to start work as a morning shift manager at a fast-food restaurant, so at 6:00 a.m., the alarm went off. The alarm was the song "If I Die Young" by The Band Perry. My partner scrambled out of bed, trying to turn the phone off before I heard too many of the lyrics. I had never heard the song before. We went into the kitchen, and our niece was up, unable to sleep. She had been one of my daughter's best friends. We told her what happened, and she said, "She spent the night at my house the night before last, and that was not her alarm ringtone." That was a sign I couldn't argue with. I knew at that moment she was okay. The question then became how was I going to be?

The next month consisted of nonstop crying. Consumed with guilt, I had sunk into a deep depression. I was going through the motions of a life but was completely numb. I looked at my partner and said, "I don't know if I'm going to make it through this. I need to talk to someone." I had attended therapy before 2010, working through anxiety and relationship issues in the past, but I had moved and never established a new provider. I wanted to find someone I could talk to who would know how I felt or had been through what I was experiencing. I called several therapists at random in my area, and each time, I had to describe to someone on the phone what had happened and why I was reaching out. After three calls, it was too painful. Luckily, my neighbor was a therapist and thought I might connect with someone she recommended.

I was terrified walking into that office for the first time. I felt as though the initial meeting was a make-or-break situation for me. I needed that person to be real, present, open, and provide a safe space. She did that. Thankfully, she had not experienced what I had gone through, but she was a mom herself, and she got it. She walked that painful journey with me, I'm sure confronting her most innate fear as a mother through my grief. It took time to build trust with my therapist. There were so many sessions when I couldn't stop crying long enough to talk. I needed to say things out loud that I wasn't willing to at first. I had so many regrets and carried so much guilt. In response to those unspoken words that I kept choking on, my therapist asked if I would trust her to close my eyes and follow her prompts. Although I didn't want to, I let her walk me through a guided imagery scenario in which I met up with my daughter and conversed with her. That was one of the most positive and powerful experiences of my therapy and a true turning point for me. I learned the power of meditation and visualization.

Approximately eight months into therapy, I realized that I had not been living the proverbial dream. I found intention and meaning through the work and self-discovery I was doing with my therapist. I discovered that I had been given the gift of perspective through my grief journey. I had survived the most painful experience I would ever have in this lifetime. I was awakened and empowered. I wanted to help others work through their grief. I went to college and completed my graduate degree in clinical and counseling psychology in 2016. I am now a certified grief counselor and am privileged to spend time with people who trust me, in their most vulnerable states, to be that safe space for them. I am honoring my daughter and living the dream.

Bio

Chris Turpyn was born and raised in Rochester, New York. The youngest of three children, her parents divorced when she was thirteen. Chris lived with her father and persevered through high school, graduating with honors, but there wasn't money available for college at the time. She had her only child at the age of twenty and through hard work, was running an information technology department for a national photography supply company by the age of twenty-three. She left that position for a better opportunity in affordable housing and had a successful career, reaching executive-level management. In 2010, her daughter died suddenly and unexpectedly. Chris struggled with grief following the death and started grief therapy. Through that journey, she realized her strong desire to help others. Chris went to college and completed her graduate degree in clinical and counseling psychology in 2016. Chris spent the first several years of her professional career in the treatment of eating disorders. She left that specialty in 2021 to pursue her passion and currently works as a certified grief counselor in honor of her daughter. Chris currently lives in Denver, Colorado, with her partner. She is a licensed therapist working remotely in the states of Colorado and Florida. Contact her at chris.turpyn@gmail.com.

Chapter 38

Awakening

By Chantalle Ullett

Throughout my life, I always felt a sense of not quite fitting in, as if I hadn't found my true home. As time passed, growing older and accumulating a myriad of experiences, a shift occurred within me. I started to listen to the subtle whispers of my inner self, embarking on a path of self-discovery that I now hold immense gratitude for. This journey involved shattering long-held belief systems that, upon closer inspection, held no truths about who I truly am. Thus, an awakening occurred.

It's not uncommon for people to have a strong sense of connection to certain places they visit, feeling as though they have a deep, almost spiritual connection to them. Some might describe this feeling as a sense of déjà vu, while others might attribute it to past life experiences or a deeper connection with the energy and history of the place. These feelings are subjective and personal. They can be a source of great inspiration and reflection.

Many cultures and belief systems have concepts related to past lives and reincarnation, which suggest that the soul can experience multiple lifetimes in different bodies and locations. While these ideas are not universally accepted, they have been deeply ingrained in many people's beliefs throughout history.

Your experiences and feelings are valid and meaningful to you and can contribute to your personal growth and self-discovery. Whether it's a genuine past-life connection or simply a strong resonance with certain places due to your own life experiences. It's an important part of your journey. Exploring these feelings and the knowledge and growth you've gained from your travels can help you better understand yourself and your place in the world. It's ultimately a personal and spiritual journey, and you should embrace it in a way that feels right for you.

In this lifetime, I've been truly blessed and fortunate to heed the whispers of my inner calling, as some may call it. Since 2015, my journey has been one of continuous exploration, a quest for knowledge, personal growth, and self-healing. It has led me to diverse corners of the world, from the enchanting landscapes of South Africa to the tranquil shores of Indonesia, the historical streets of the Czech Republic, the ancient wonders of Egypt, and the vast expanse of both Canada and the United States.

Throughout these remarkable journeys, an amazing revelation unfolded. It was as though a part of my very being had already traversed these lands in times long past. My soul seemed to bear the imprints of lives once lived in these places. To some, this idea may seem outlandish, even bordering on the fantastical, and I understand that. But I cannot deny what I've felt, sensed, and witnessed during my physical presence in these locales.

For me, it's a deeply personal truth that transcends skepticism. It's as if the echoes of bygone eras resonate within my very being when I've stood in these sacred spots, whispering secrets of a past that has left an indelible mark on my present. While some might dismiss it as musings of a dreamer or the flights of an imaginative mind, I carry with the unwavering conviction of a traveler who has unearthed a profound connection between the world and the spirits of the places I've been privileged to visit. When I set foot in these remarkable places, I was not merely a tourist; I was an observer of my existence. Each journey became a profound quest to unravel layers of my being, a journey into the depths of self-awareness.

I hold a steadfast belief that nothing in life happens by mere chance. There are no coincidences, only purposeful encounters. It's as though my inner self possesses an innate knowledge that we have trodden upon their very grounds before. Some might attribute this sensation to the concept of reincarnation, a belief deeply rooted within my core. I carry vivid recollections of toiling on land and sea, harmoniously coexisting with the animals, and even the most astounding of all, a profound sense of where my initial life began. The remarkable part is that these are places I've set foot in during this lifetime, places I never physically visited before.

One such place was in the heart of South Africa, where I embarked on a *solo* adventure, so to speak. My journey unfolded with a group of fellow explorers/observers, and amid the myriad excursions, two experiences etched themselves into the fabric of my memories.

One day, we ventured to Adam's Calendar, a sacred site cloaked in mystery. As I stood upon a flat rock to the side of Towering Pillars akin to Stonehenge, an unexpected journey began. The moment my feet touched that ancient stone, the boundaries of time and space blurred, transporting me to a distant era. I found myself enslaved, toiling in the pursuit of gold for enigmatic beings, acknowledged by some and denied by others. The surroundings felt hauntingly familiar, as if I had stepped back into a life lived long ago. How could a place I had never physically known evoke such a profound sense of home?

My other memorable experience unfolded in North Kruger Park, a day filled with driving across the vast expanse of the park in search of the sentient beings society simply calls animals. The day proved to be exceptionally fortunate, offering us numerous en- counters with the incredible wildlife—a true blessing.

As we were wrapping up our day and preparing to de- part the park, our attention was drawn to an elephant discreetly positioned behind a bush. We decided to stop and take a moment to observe and establish a heart-to-heart connection with this magnificent be- ing. In that tranquil exchange, something remarkable happened.

Later in the day, my friend Andre approached me, cu- rious about what I had observed and felt during our interaction with the elephant. As I tried to articulate my experience, I could only express a vague sense of familiarity, an intuitive feeling that lingered without a clear explanation. It wasn't until after I had expressed this that he mentioned noticing and feeling a strong bond between the elephant and me.

It wasn't until 6 months later that the pieces of this puzzle fell into place. Through past life regression, it was revealed that the elephant and I shared a bonded lifetime together. The majestic beast, hidden behind the bush, had somehow sensed and recognized our connection. The revelation was nothing short of a mind-blowing testament to the mysterious and intricate threads that connect us across time and existence.

In those contrasting experiences, one mystical and the other rooted in the untamed wilderness, South Africa revealed itself as a land of paradoxes. A place where the past whispered through ancient stones and the present roared with the wild heartbeat of the African Bush. My journey became a story woven with threads of disbelief, awe, and profound connection to a land that held more mysteries than I could fathom.

Little did I know or understand that my experience in South Africa was just the beginning of a profound journey to understanding the depth of my being. It's fascinating how complex humans truly are. The journey began with an awareness and awakening, a deep-seated yearning to explore and discover more about myself unknowingly—an understanding that we are more than just our physical selves. There's a higher power within all of us, something waiting to be uncovered, but often, we're simply asleep to it.

My life, once familiar, underwent a profound transformation. What I knew, and how I know it, is no longer the same. This journey, in many ways, feels like it's just begun, and for that, I am eternally grateful. It's a journey into the depths of self-awareness, a constant unraveling of layers that reveal the essence of my existence. Each revelation marks a step forward, and as I navigate this unfolding path, the sense of gratitude deepens for the awakening that has set my soul on a course of profound discovery.

Bio

Chantalle's sessions are characterized by personal synergies treatments that integrate advanced breathwork techniques, bodywork modalities, and the unique approaches of Linking Awareness and the Bodytalk System. Her expertise extends beyond traditional massage therapy, offering a holistic approach that addresses the whole person. Whether working with humans or sentient beings such as horses, cats, dogs, orangutans, elephants, and dolphins, Chantalle's transformative healings reflect her deep understanding of the interconnectedness of the body, mind, and spirit.

With a profound commitment to facilitating lasting well-being, Chantalle Ullett stands as a beacon in the field of holistic healing, providing individuals with an opportunity for comprehensive and transformative care.

You can connect with Chantalle via,
www.breathinglifetherapeutics.com
cullett72@att.net

Chapter 39

Rising from the Ashes

By Wanda Vitale

Sixty wasn't supposed to be like this. A full leg brace after an accident, a terrifying diagnosis, a depleted bank account, no income, no spouse or family, and no help in sight. How could this be? Sitting at my dining room table, looking upward, I said: "You win. I give up. Whatever I decided my life would be before I took on this body, *you win*. If it means being homeless and lame, *you win*."

I had two choices: do what I said I knew, or suicide. I had so many memories of other lives where life was anything but pleasant. The toothless old beggar stoned to death in some ancient village. A woman who died a painful death in some cold English slum. A nurse in France during World War I overcome with depression after her entire family was killed in the war. She drowned herself, and I experienced the drowning over and over in recurring dreams as a kid.

What if the next time was worse? So, I surrendered. Not to some outside source like God or in hopelessness. I surrendered to anything and everything known.

Death would have felt easier.

Little did I know then that this moment would be the moment when everything changed and when I would never look back.

My life had not been easy with no real security, always pushing the limits. But this? I couldn't go back to my old life in software because I was too old. I could barely walk. I still had seven foreclosures from investments after the real estate crash. I had $134 in my bank account and my electric bill was $168, and I had absolutely no idea what to do. That's saying something since my entire life was about being responsible, being in charge, and being smart and successful.

And being in control.

Our soul does whatever it needs to do to wake us up to our power and bring us the life we decided upon before we took on these bodies.

How did I get to this very uncomfortable place in my life? I'd done all the right things. I was always responsible, taking on a career where there were very few women, and somehow always being at the top of the sales producers list. I did whatever was necessary to be successful and persisted. Yet, I never fit in. I wasn't competitive. Unlike my colleagues, living a lavish life didn't drive me. I had other interests that were out of place in this dog-eat-dog world of competition and ego.

I began questioning religion, the nature of reality, and what people called 'the metaphysical' as a teenager. A friend and I started driving to the nearest city to see psychics as soon as we could drive. I immersed myself in the channeled material from Jane Roberts, the entity known as Seth, who spoke in detail, and at a college level, about the nature of reality. Later, I would study A *Course in Miracles*, channeling, and just about everything else I could get my hands on.

But it was just philosophy that filled my life on the weekends after my work week, while I persisted in creating a life I thought would make me happy. There was one small problem: there was none of *me* in it. The real me.

I was always in control in some way. I was smart, capable, and I learned early on that I could trust myself to do just about anything. I could push that nagging fear down like a poker player and never face it, while my mind devised some brilliant strategy that would get me through the next hurdle. Where was my heart in all this? Not there. I didn't realize that life was supposed to feel good. Growing up in a dysfunctional family as an empath, receiving love or attention was not my experience. At the time, I had no idea that life was *meant* to be kind. Grace? What was that? Fear had been my faithful friend for decades, a heart-crushing fear that slammed my body and drowned out any hint of inspiration and guidance. I had completely ignored the soul nudges and kept plodding along the narrative I believed would eventually yield happiness.

Before that day at my dining room table, I had recurring dreams where I stood in front of a firing squad. I'd wake up just before the guns went off. Finally, one night, I stood not six feet in front of a man with a gun pointed at my chest. There was nowhere to go, and I realized my death was inevitable. The loud 'bang' of the gun sounded. There was smoke everywhere, and yet I was still alive. My body was still intact. As I looked at the gun, I saw a flag in the barrel that said: "Bang!" What a sense of humor my wise soul had!

It all collapsed in that moment at my dining room table when I said yes to the possibility of being homeless and lame in Phoenix in the searing heat. In that moment, any sense of control or resistance was gone. My body went limp, then relaxed after all those years of attempting to control the life force that was here to live through me, as me.

The next day, you-can't-make-this-stuff-up things began to happen: a session with a gifted seer who could see my energetic probabilities that I couldn't at the time. My guides, who I realize now are aspects of me, began coming through louder and louder with guidance. While I had learned a lot, and amassed information over the decades, that big wall of fear had prevented me from implementing any action. So I did.

One day at a time, I trusted the life force that was so much bigger and knew so much more than my little mind did. Every morning, I would ask, 'What are we doing today?' And I did it, no matter how irrational or how much fear I felt. There were massive financial and health challenges to work through, and somehow, step by step, week by week, everything changed. I was shown how to work energetically with my body, and my health normalized. Information poured in from other realms (of me) to start a group, to use what I knew to help others. Money came in from the most unexpected sources, a few hundred thousand dollars from an inheritance that wasn't even from family. Five years ago, I met a wonderful man who adores me, and we married.

Fast-forward to today, ten years or so after the final surrender. My longtime friend, fear, and its cousins, doubt and anxiety, left the house for good. Life feels so fulfilling and I love my life! The events that led to my surrender were my Ph.D. for the work I do with others who are ready for a life of fulfillment and freedom. All those years ago, I learned that our beliefs create our physical reality, but now my in-depth experience of the nuts and bolts is the foundation for helping others who are empathic materialize their dreams.

With our highly attuned senses, and with a little assistance around boundaries and self-love, we are particularly wired for this new age when the world is coming to realize a new truth. Everything is created twice: first in imagination with our feeling sense, and then it materializes in the world of form.

We are the ones the world has been waiting for.

We're imagining a completely new world based on heart-centered wisdom, accessing the wisdom beyond the mind's reach. We each play an integral role in the greatest acceleration this planet has ever experienced.

There is something that only you can contribute, whether it's as a pattern-breaker, a healer, or embodying a new way of being. Your heart holds the key. If my story has offered any value, let it be to surrender to the life force that's ready to live *you*, that knows exactly what it's doing. Your life until now has been the education required. That life force in you has a built-in plan and path, and the only thing preventing it from loving and guiding you is fear. And a little control.

If I can do it, anyone can. Notice the soul nudges. Follow your heart. Create a life you love. Say yes to your dreams. You're here for a reason grander than our little minds can begin to fathom.

Bio

Wanda Vitale guides men and women to follow their hearts to create a life of meaning and fulfillment. She is a mainstream corporate exec turned practical mystic, blending the best of both in her work as a certified life coach. Wanda consistently guides her clients to turn their biggest, illogical dreams into the lives they wake up to each day—the easy way. You can find her hiking in the mountains and enjoying motorcycle trips with her husband. Learn more at: www.theempoweredempaths.com

Chapter 40

Cutting the Cord

By Michelyn Woityra

M oments after a baby is born into this world, one of the first things that happens is the cutting of the umbilical cord. Symbolically, this action breaks the link from the baby's internal womb, which allows them to be separated and on their own for the first time.

Throughout life, you have heard the saying, "*Cut the cord.*" Which can translate into, move on, let it go. These three words can be powerful. They were for me.

Just to give you a glimpse of where this all began. My healthy relationship radar was off. I had two failed marriages by the time I was 32. My first marriage was with a man who married me because I was battling cancer. After 7 years, we parted because we wanted different things out of life. My second marriage was to a man that I had known since I was a young teenager. The day after we said our vows, the verbal and physical abuse started, and the lifetime nightmare I was trapped in began. I could not go anywhere without him. I was put down and made to feel less than on a daily basis, and I learned quickly to walk with my head down and not to make eye contact with anyone, especially another man. If I did any of this, I would feel the wrath when we were alone. I had moved to California, so I did not have any friends or family to turn to. After a year of this abuse, I planned my escape. One weekend, while he was on a military mission, I packed my car up, left my keys and wedding ring on the table, and embarked on a six-day drive back to Florida.

After fleeing back to Florida, the last thing on my mind was another relationship. I was mentally and emotionally broken and dealing with PTSD. I lived in fear that my estranged husband would come back for me, and although I was physically safe, internally, a tornado was spinning. I was always looking over my shoulder, not able to make eye contact with anyone. I had nothing to offer another person, and it felt like healing was eons away.

About 8 months after I returned home, I reconnected with a man that I went to high school with. I still had the walls up, but something felt different. He was kindhearted, and his presence made me feel safe, but red flags were waving, and I was putting on my blinders again. He was always in between jobs, he had no transportation, and he had to couch surf with no real home to call his own. So, what do I do? I rented an apartment, cosigned on a vehicle, and started to take care of him financially. The abuse and constant cheating started to peek its ugly head about a year in, and my heart was filled with a lot of anger and sadness. Another toxic cycle that I was aware of. This relationship went on for about 3 years when one day, while I was taking a walk with my eight-year-old son, it hit me. Is this who I wanted as a role model for my son? Is this what I want in a partner? I was a single mom with a solid career and wanted more out of life. I needed more out of life, so a week later, I broke things off.

My new beginning was exciting. My son and I moved into a beautiful condominium. I was thriving and felt that a huge weight had been lifted. Life felt lighter, at least for a few months. Then, my newfound happiness started to turn bleak. One night, I answered a text from my ex, and that turned into us spending time together and me once again taking care of him financially. The toxic cycle was in front of me, and this time, I knew exactly what I was getting into.

Then, one beautiful April day in 2015 happened that changed everything. I was meeting my mentor Beth downtown, which is something we would do monthly. We would get coffee and walk to the park, where we would meditate. Beth was a sounding board for me and someone I had the utmost respect for. Our time together was always enlightening. She played a huge role in the healing process from my past. Taking an hour from the busyness of life brought serenity internally. This day, though, was different and one I will never forget. Beth and I spent about fifteen minutes meditating, and then we felt the presence of these two squirrels that were chasing each other up a tree. Beth did not like squirrels. I thought they were adorable, so we decided to move our blanket.

Beth always sensed when things were heavy on my heart, so she asked me what was going on. I opened up to her, admitting I was seeing my ex, and started helping him financially again. I felt guilty for his situation. Beth then said something extremely *profound* to me. "Michelyn, you need to cut the cord."

She started to explain that the universe is responding to my energy. If I want to bring happiness and love into my heart, I need to sever the ties with my ex and manifest exactly what I wanted. So, I did. On my way home from the park, I called my ex and cut the cord. I then went home to write a letter to the universe. I had nothing to lose. Clearly, when it came to relationships, my way never served me.

I found myself on my balcony. The sun was starting to set, and I was at peace and excited. I sat still and began writing my list to the universe. A kind heart, Christian, single father, goal-oriented, did not drink, smoke, or do drugs. Someone who was adventurous loved the outdoors. I even went as far as the color of his eyes. When I was done, I had a list of 33 non-negotiables that I sealed and put in my journal.

The universe works quickly. It had been about ten days since I cut the cord. I decided to check my Christian Mingle account before bed. I had set one up just to prove to myself that my intentions of profoundly moving on and not getting wrapped up in old toxic habits were pure. I had messages, most I deleted, and then I came across one that caught my eye. His smile drew me in. I read his profile, and it felt as if we had a lot in common, so I sent a wave back.

The next morning, I found out that the man who would end up turning my world upside down's name was Matt. Matt was a vet and served in the Marines, which in the past would have made me run. He checked off all but one of the lists I had written to the universe. We started a whirlwind romance. It started with long, detailed conversations through email for about two weeks. Emails transpired into phone calls at night after our kids were sleeping. On June 25, 2015, we met in person, and the moment Matt embraced me in a hug, I knew he was the one that I would spend my forever with.

Cutting the cord precisely at that moment changed the course of my life. If I had not taken Beth's advice that day, I would not be where I am today. I am blessed with someone who values me as a person. I feel seen, safe, and loved. Matt and I thrive in life together. In 2016, we welcomed a healthy boy into this world. In 2020, Matt proposed to me in front of a zebra exhibit at our favorite zoo, and later that year, we married under this huge oak tree at our favorite park by Beth's husband. It was simple and magical. Just the two of us.

Now, I do not want to fool anyone into thinking what Matt and I have is perfect; it takes work. I had to heal from past traumas. I am a work in progress. Spiritually, I am growing all the time, and I give everything over to my higher power. My life is filled with gratitude, and anytime I can, I pay it forward and remind others that asking the universe and manifesting that life you desire can happen. Sometimes, it just takes cutting the cord.

Bio

Michelyn Woityra is a devoted wife, mother, empath, and entrepreneur. She is a passionate writer with a children's book in progress. Balancing home-schooling her young son Chase and supporting her eldest son Mirko's journey along with running a small crafting business, she exemplifies dedication in both family and creative endeavors. As a two-time cancer survivor, she embraces life and focuses on spreading light, love, and positivity into this world. Her inspiring journey reflects the harmonious fusion of nurturing and pursuing her dreams.

Michelyn can be reached by email at: iheartgnomesandmore@gmail.com.

Chapter 41

Navigating Manifestation's Messy Middle

By Janet Zavala

As I fly cross-country from California to North Carolina, I find myself in the realization stage of a 10-year manifestation journey. I'm facilitating a workshop appropriately titled *Embrace Your Full Potential* as I step into mine.

It's exciting when your dreams become reality. What people don't see, however, is manifestation's messy middle, the space between the inception and arrival of your dreams. It's a challenging phase, filled with obstacles and trauma that make returning to the comfort zone tempting.

When you reach the manifestation stage, you can see threads of synchronicity. From this vantage point, you begin to understand the lessons manufactured for your benefit, no matter how unwelcome at the time. I climbed out of my messy middle to encourage you to hold onto your dreams even when it seems the world is conspiring against you. If you're beginning your journey, understand that the messy middle will arrive unexpectedly. If the messy middle made you abandon your dreams, it's not too late to reflect on the lessons and restart your journey.

Clarity Starts to Form

My dreams started to materialize when I discovered the coaching profession during a failed attempt to earn a graduate degree. Coaching, once a brief segment in multi-day leadership training, became a passion as I witnessed its transformative impact on people's lives. As a manager in a large corporation, I integrated coaching into my role while navigating an unclear economic path toward entrepreneurship as a single mother in her forties, saving for retirement.

- **Synchronicity**. Coaching an employee on the verge of termination, I realized his issues weren't from a lack of effort or desire. His unique way of processing information wasn't appreciated (and often not tolerated) in corporations. He couldn't conform to the standards of thinking and behaving frequently rewarded. During our weekly conversations, I was able to flex my newly developed skills. Together, we developed an approach to his job that not only worked for him but allowed him to excel as his confidence grew.

- **Manifestation Moment.** Finding a way in a safe environment to improve my skills allowed me to deepen my love for the craft, get good at it, and develop clarity about how I wanted to evolve. You signal to the universe your desires when you dream big and reaffirm your dreams through consistent action.

Opportunity Shows Up

Dreaming big and taking consistent action attracts more opportunities. Presenting ideas to infuse coaching into workplace activities and leading a women's empowerment group opened doors. For the next five years, I created dozens of workshops, delivering empowering content to hundreds of employees.

- **Synchronicity**. The perfect series of events will occur at the right time. My destiny required me to accept the lead role of the women's group because I needed that experience to accept the opportunity seven years later in North Carolina.

- **Manifestation Moment.** The universe steps in to provide you with the right opportunities when you're ready. You simply need to say yes.

Distractions

As my day job got busier and I continued to lead our women's group, I started to conceptualize the book I wanted to write. I channeled my professional passions in these areas. Even as my day job got more stressful, it was my favorite work era. I led a team I loved dearly. As we worked late into the night, we were bonded by our dedication and strong relationships.

With the visibility I received for my job and the women's group, I was asked by high-ranking leaders to apply for a promotion. I cried uncontrollably when I told my team I got the job. The tears and the overwhelming foreboding should have been a warning. I was physically moving from the 2nd floor to the 3rd, yet it felt like I was moving miles away. I didn't want the promotion, yet the change felt pre-ordained. The worst 18 months of my professional career began as I was flung into manifestation's messy middle.

- **Synchronicity**. I wasn't paying attention to my big dreams. My sense of comfort dulled my urgency. When your dreams start to slip through your hands, foregoing them becomes a viable option. The uphill climb appears in-surmountable. You settle into the thought, "I can live with this," as an alternative to pursu-ing your goals.

- **Manifestation Moment**. The universe does not like it when you give up on your dreams. She presents two paths. One path is to set-tle for less than you are capable of, but may be safe and easy. The alternative is harder to navigate but will ultimately lead to the destiny you were intended to reach.

The Redirection

Eighteen horrific months were coming to an end in mid-2020, but not before some final gut punches. I injured my back, and work was torturing me in ways I could never imagine. The final blow came when my former employee, only 45 years old, lost her battle with a relentless type of cancer. I was depressed and convinced I would lose my job. Most days, I couldn't stop crying or get out of bed.

Miracles from angels in human form materialized. A former manager intervened on my behalf. This gave me enough courage to reach out to my previous group, begging that manager to bring me back into the safe embrace of the group I love. A deal was made, and I returned to my old group. My ego was bruised. I felt like a failure until I was shown the universe's plan. Ultimately, that manager orchestrated the opportunity in North Carolina.

Another angel entered my life when I joined an online course. He told me about an opportunity to get published as part of a compilation book. He introduced me to As You Wish Publishing, the publishers of this book you're reading now. I shelved my own book years ago as I struggled through the messy middle. Slowly, the light began to shine on my path forward.

- **Synchronicity.** When I didn't have the strength or confidence to ask for help, people around me noticed I needed it. Look out for angels in human form. They are all around you.

- **Manifestation Moment.** Your life will fall apart in service of you. When you've lost your way, the universe's only recourse is to tear your life apart brick by brick so you can rise out of the rubble and start rebuilding. Through the falling apart you can discard what no longer serves you. And through the rebuilding, you begin to witness the strength you have through a new lens.

The Moving Forward

I had the space, time, and support I needed to heal from the trauma and pain. I rediscovered my passions and embraced my talents and strengths. I noticed the synchronicities and threads that existed between all my experiences. Unfortunately, they are often only visible in hindsight. At any point along my journey, I could have let the trauma derail my dreams. The universe had a plan, and I had the choice to either accept the plan or give up on my dreams.

I decided to step into the full potential of what my life could become. The universe cannot manifest a reality that you don't fully believe is possible. The universe wants the magic you have to offer. She will lay out the opportunities, expose you to the right information at the right time, and introduce you to the people you need to meet to make it a reality. She will create a diversion to get you back on the path. You must be willing to step into the magic. Your cooperation is required.

If it feels like the manifestation of your dreams is impossible, please know that the universe has not forgotten you. You may be in the comfort zone of your old life or the messy middle of your own manifestation. You have a choice; you can follow the guidance or give up on the dream of what your life could become. Use these prompts to reflect on your manifestation journey.

- Identify the threads of synchronicity in your experiences.

- What have been your biggest lessons?

- What strengths have you uncovered?

- What expectations do you need to let go of?

In the center of my current manifestation, I'm not attached to a specific outcome. I expect success while acknowledging disappointments will arise. I have the strength and knowledge to persevere. Manifestation's messy middle doesn't need to end your journey; release comfort, heal wounds, and embrace the magic by developing clarity, trusting the universe and yourself, and expressing gratitude for your life.

Bio

Janet is a Certified Empowerment Coach, and a Workshop Creator and Facilitator. She is a 4-time best-selling author of *The Nature of Transformation*and three compilation books. She is passionate about empowering women to navigate life and career transitions, discover their true potential, and create a life they love. Visit JanetZavalaCoaching.com to contact Janet and learn more about her services.

🌟 Unlock Your Writing Potential with As You Wish Publishing! 🌟

Are you an aspiring author with a story to share? As You Wish Publishing invites you to join our self-help collaboration books and embark on a journey to becoming a published author!

✨ Why Choose As You Wish Publishing?

- Collaborative Magic: We believe in the power of collective creativity! Our collaborative approach makes publishing accessible to first-time authors, fostering a supportive community.
- Guided Assistance: Fear not if you're new to the world of publishing! Our expert team provides step-by-step guidance, ensuring a smooth and enjoyable experience for writers of all levels.
- Diverse Voices: Embrace the richness of diverse perspectives. Join a vibrant community of writers who share their unique stories, creating books that resonate with a wide range of readers.
- Professional Quality: Your story deserves to shine! As You Wish Publishing maintains high standards of quality, delivering professionally produced books that you can proudly share with the world.

🎉 Join As You Wish Publishing Today!

Ready to make your mark in the world of publishing? Don't miss this opportunity to become a published author with As You Wish Publishing. Embrace collaboration, unlock your writing potential, and share your story with the world!

📧 email us at connect@asyouwishpublishing.com to start your publishing journey today.
Visit us at www.asyouwishpublishing.com for more information and to submit your story.

Made in United States
North Haven, CT
13 February 2024

48565438R10163